Kevin McGarry

Fatherhood for Gay Men
An Emotional and Practical Guide to Becoming a Gay Dad

Pre-publication
REVIEWS,
COMMENTARIES,
EVALUATIONS . . .

"McGarry, a natural dad, questions whether he should adopt as a gay single man. We are privileged to glimpse into his rich emotional life as he takes us through the nail-biting process of adopting in Vietnam. This book is an affirming and practical guide for the lucky reader who wants to learn how to adopt, whether you are gay or not.

McGarry finds his authentic self and becomes emotionally happier as he realizes his dream of becoming a father, not once, but twice."

Linda R. Brownlee, LCSW
Director of the Adoption Center
of Washington

"Kevin McGarry does an excellent job of describing the emotional roller coaster of becoming a single gay adoptive parent. His twice-taken journey has touched many of us, and he has encouraged many gay men and women to consider how their lives would be enriched as the parents of a little boy or girl. It is frank and revealing and will help prospective gay parents understand the benefits and challenges of parenthood. It also accurately describes the often laborious paperwork process involved in this journey, which can be overwhelming and discouraging at times. This book is an indispensable tool for those who are considering or in the process of adopting as gay parents. Kevin should be commended for putting this very personal journey on paper to share with those who would also want to travel this road."

John M. Coster, PhD
Adoptive gay father

More pre-publication
REVIEWS, COMMENTARIES, EVALUATIONS . . .

"I only regret that Kevin McGarry's honest, searching, and comprehensive guide wasn't around when my partner and I were adopting. For readers embarking on their own parenting adventure, *Fatherhood for Gay Men* is a mother lode of inside knowledge and, equally important, a wellspring of hope. It's a book written from and to the heart."

Louis Bayard
Author, *Fool's Errand*
and *Endangered Species*

─────※─────

"By taking a progressive approach in *Fatherhood for Gay Men: An Emotional and Practical Guide to Becoming a Gay Dad,* McGarry offers very realistic insight into the thinking and the processes involved in becoming a gay dad in today's society. In walking the reader through the various stages of his own adoption process in a foreign country, McGarry provides both a financial and emotional picture of what one can expect. He clearly presents the emotional ups and downs as well as the eventual triumphs that occur as one begins and passes through the journey to forming a family. This book would have been a tremendous help in dealing with the various starts and stops awaiting us in our own adoption process.

The chapter, "My Journey to Vietnam," clearly a highlight of the book, is narrated using the journal McGarry kept during his trip. The entries, filled with all of the emotions and uncertainties of being in a foreign country, unfold here. The vivid pictures painted of the people around him, as well as the events in the adoption, make this chapter especially touching and give you a forthright view of one man's journey into forming his family."

Bob Page
Founder and CEO,
Replacements, Ltd.

Dale Frederiksen
VP of Product Information,
Replacements, Ltd.

Harrington Park Press®
An Imprint of The Haworth Press, Inc.
New York • London • Oxford

Fatherhood for Gay Men

An Emotional and Practical Guide to Becoming a Gay Dad

Fatherhood for Gay Men
An Emotional and Practical Guide to Becoming a Gay Dad

Kevin McGarry

HPP

Harrington Park Press®
An Imprint of The Haworth Press, Inc.
New York • London • Oxford

Published by

Harrington Park Press®, an imprint of The Haworth Press, Inc., 10 Alice Street, Binghamton, NY 13904-1580.

Cover painting by Laureen E. McGarry.

Cover design by Lora Wiggins.

Library of Congress Cataloging-in-Publication Data

McGarry, K. P.
    Fatherhood for gay men : an emotional and practical guide to becoming a gay dad / Kevin McGarry.
        p. cm.
    ISBN 1-56023-387-7 (hardcover : alk. paper) — ISBN 1-56023-388-5 (softcover : alk. paper)
    1. Gay fathers. 2. Gay adoption. 3. McGarry, K. J. I. Title.
HQ76.13 .M343 2003
306.874'2—dc21

                                                                                    2002012133

7|06

This book is dedicated to Kevin Lee Johnson.
When you spoke of your dreams of adopting a child,
you always said "when," not "if."
Kevin, you would have been a great father.

ABOUT THE AUTHOR

Kevin McGarry, an accountant by trade, is also the author of "Antic-ipating Andrew," a short story of his first meeting with the older of his two adopted sons.

CONTENTS

Foreword

The first time I heard of the "Gayby Boom" was in 1990 at a millennium panel of the American Psychological Association, predicting sociological trends and the mental health needs for the gay community of the next decade and into the future. Lesbians had already been having babies and creating families, and gay men were in the midst of the AIDS crisis and talk of babies seemed far-reaching. Since that time, the gay community has evolved in significant ways. The community as a whole has made great strides in coming out of the closet and being more visible throughout society. Our political presence is now felt nationally and gay issues are becoming commonplace throughout mainstream culture and the media. As more individuals have become empowered by living lives out in the open, the number of gay men who have decided to become fathers is increasing. Although still only a small subsection of the gay community, their presence is growing. More young gay men today are considering parenthood and have begun to think of having children as a viable option. The publication of this volume is timely as it meets an emerging need within the gay community. Its day has come.

This book is both a touching personal account and a valuable, pragmatic, how-to guide for those gay men considering adoption. The memoirs are filled with emotion and convey the struggles for one man, who single-handedly has been able to make his dream of fatherhood come to reality. The book also provides a comprehensive outline of how one can move through the adoption process, providing useful tips and helpful information to consider. The author is a very grounded individual and speaks with a voice that is psychologically sophisticated, offering his readers sound and wise advice. When I adopted my son in 1996 there were very few gay men to turn to as a role model, so at the time I felt a bit like a gay pioneer. I would have wished for a book such as this one to help guide me through the process of considering parenthood and adoption. Mr. McGarry has captured the essence of being a father and is a wonderful role model for any gay man considering parenthood.

Gordon Cohen, PsyD
Clinical Psychologist;
Co-Director, Affirmative
Psychotherapy Group,
Washington, DC

Preface

"Why don't I have two daddies?" asked my son Andy one day, while we were talking about a friend of his who has two dads. If, as they say, truth comes from the mouths of babes, Andy's innocent question was a comment on a new world for families. Andy's concept of families at age four is that some have two daddies or two mommies, some have one daddy or one mommy, and some have a daddy and a mommy. His perception of family is already the way I envisioned it would be—that each is unique. I see this as a gift from which he'll benefit rather than a burden he will have to bear.

I have adopted two Vietnamese boys, Andrew and Vincent. This book is the story of my emotional journey to fatherhood. It is also a practical guide for gay men who are considering parenthood, whether single or partnered. I wrote it for two reasons: first, to encourage gay men who might have parental instincts to take the risks (and enjoy the rewards) involved with adoption and, second, because I have seen many children in need of good homes. As you will see in the following pages, matching parent with child and processing the related paperwork seems simple compared to what I went through emotionally in making the decision to adopt—even for the second time. It is my hope that this book will assist gay men in their pursuit of fatherhood and, most important, a few more children in need will grow up in loving homes.

Special thanks to Paul Albergo, Lisa Bennett, Gordon Cohen, Gillian Dunne, John Edwards, Michael Gordon, Patrick Kanary, David Leary, Laureen McGarry, and John Parkhurst for your assistance, inspiration, and encouragement. This book would have been utterly incomplete without each of you.

Chapter 1

Closet Daddy

Andrew and I were on a five-hour flight to Las Vegas the day he turned twenty-two months old. It was our first plane trip since our flight from Vietnam seventeen months earlier. The plane was completely full; we had one aisle seat for the two of us. About an hour before the plane landed, an elderly woman who had been sitting in the row behind us approached me and said she admired how I cared for my son. I thanked her, and she responded that fathers' roles sure have changed since she raised her children. I wondered . . . What was I doing that would make a total stranger comment on my parenting skills? Whatever it was, her generous words were encouraging. This kind of encouragement, even well after adopting, helps me affirm my place as a father. I constantly feel privileged and lucky to be a dad, although, as the title of this chapter suggests, it took me a while to get there. My path to fatherhood was as emotionally difficult as had been my coming out as a gay man many years earlier. In my heart I knew I was a natural dad, but intellectually I had to convince myself that I could do it. I believe the gut feelings we all have are a window into the way in which we really want to live our lives, but we are often restrained by societal or family pressures. We take risks by coming out of the closet as gay men, and at the end of the day, we are emotionally happier because we took those risks. By coming out, we are being true to who we are. The same goes for anyone, gay or straight, who has gut instincts for parenthood. I knew over the years that I had parenting instincts because I had this incredible envy of other dads. I would watch them with their kids and wish that somehow I could have that role. It was painful at times because, being gay, I didn't think parenting was in my life plan. Had more role models been available to me, the process would have been a little less difficult—the closet door would have opened easier this time.

As I look back, the adoption process (preparing seemingly endless paperwork, traveling to Vietnam for extended stays, and parting with large sums of money) was much easier than the emotional decision to become a parent. I am sure that if adoption were simpler or less expensive, more people would adopt, but the decision would hold the same weight. The prospective parent would have a huge emotional hill to climb. For single adopting parents, the decision is more difficult because it is theirs and theirs alone. Perhaps couples have an easier time with such decisions because they can discuss their dreams, debate the issues involved, and plan how they will share the duties. When I was making the decision to adopt, perhaps the biggest decision of my life, I was always doubtful and uncertain, wavering right up until the moment I met Andrew—then, fait accompli.

The woman on the plane to Las Vegas was right; parenting roles have changed in recent years, but still very few men raise babies alone. Women adopt as single parents more often than men do. In fact, if you decide to adopt internationally, there are only a handful of countries that will allow single men to adopt, but most of them with adoption programs do allow single women to adopt. Many of these countries are developing countries and may not be as socially advanced as Western societies. Their traditions declare that a woman be involved in the day-to-day care of children. Luckily, a few countries support the concept that men can be primary caregivers too.

After I adopted Andrew, the transition from single gay guy to single parent was relatively easy. Soon after, I realized that it was easy because I had parental instincts. Being a gay man and being a good father are not mutually exclusive. Throughout most of the past thirty years of the gay rights movement, the focus has been on ourselves and our pride as gay men. We have delivered to ourselves the message that parenting is not a priority for us; parenting is for our straight brothers and sisters, single women, or lesbian couples. Perhaps diaper-changing gay men are the last frontier for parenting. I feel this distinction often and it makes me proud.

When I came out in 1980, I subconsciously and silently mourned the loss of parenthood. I shrugged off the notion that I wanted to be a dad someday. I reveled in my freedom of being honest with myself about my sexuality, so the mourning of my potential parenthood was drowned by sheer happiness of belonging. I lived for weekends, to go to the local gay disco to be with other gay people. This was truly a happy time for me, despite the loss I was ignoring. I treated the father inside of me as if he didn't exist. I treated my religion in much the same way. I believed that since I was gay, I could no longer be a Catholic—the two didn't mix. As a child, I grew up believing that being gay is bad. When I first came out, I still thought that way, but I had found others similar to me and so didn't feel as isolated. It took a while to build enough self-esteem to believe that most gay people deserve and are capable of spiritual lives and meaningful relationships. My spirituality did not have to suffer or go away because of who I am. From there, my self-confidence blossomed to allow me to think seriously about becoming a father. I attribute this delay to the absence of role models for gay men as fathers. Hopefully, in the next few years, gay men who are natural parents will become the fathers that they want to be—and it will be as normal for them as for any other parent.

When I first came out to myself, I was enrolled in the local Big Brother program. I struggled about it for quite some time but decided to quit because I thought they wouldn't allow a gay man in their program. I quit a volunteer activity that I truly loved and left a fatherless thirteen-year-old boy Big Brotherless without an explanation. Again, I shrugged it off as a necessary loss along the way of my becoming true to myself. I look back on that now and am sad for him and me. I made this decision based on society's judgments and my naive unfounded fears. Not only was I mourning the loss of my ever being a father, I was severing ties that were as similar to parenthood as I could get at the time. The father in me then became further entrenched in my soul than the gay man ever had been.

As the years passed, I thought more about adoption, but I always thought it was beyond my reach. I never thought adoption was an option for single people, much less for gay single people. I'd heard about a few gay couples adopting—mostly as news stories in faraway places. I admired them, but adoption still seemed so distant and uncertain. I feared that if I went through with it, someone would take the child away or allow me to get really close to adopting and then say no. Also, of course, I was waiting until I had a partner and hoping that he would have paternal instincts too. Thinking of all the time and paperwork, I considered the process insurmountable. For some reason, I thought being gay would mean more paperwork or delays. These were all fleeting thoughts, as I would never dwell on them for too long. If I did, I ran the risk of becoming depressed.

Often, whenever I would see an unfortunate child, I would say to myself, "I'll take that child and give him or her a good home. I just wish someone would let me." Whether this was a child being scolded by a mean parent in the local grocery store or a poor begging child in another country, I felt I could help and love him or her. I thought it was unfair that the world had both unwanted and unappreciated children and me, who could provide a loving home for at least one of them. Putting us together, however, seemed too difficult. How do you start? Where do you look? Again, I pushed my parenting instincts deeper inside.

Then, in 1995, a friend of mine and his partner adopted a baby boy. Although happy for them, I also felt some envy and sadness because it wasn't looking good for me ever to do the same. I had turned forty that year and was not in a relationship, and I felt that I could not parent alone. My biological clock was ticking; my chances of finding a partner soon enough to adopt a baby were getting slimmer. Eventually, I saw an article in the local gay newspaper about one man's journey to becoming a single dad. The author was the founder of an organization that held single-parent adoption workshops. I attended the next workshop, which featured a panel of four single parents telling their stories. I met others interested in adopting, and I thought, perhaps they ask themselves the same questions: "Can I do this?" "Do I want to do this?" I felt envious of the single parents on the panel, who appeared to have great kids and seemed happy in their parenting roles. On the other side of the room were we wannabe parents, almost silent, just taking it all in. While learning about the large volume of paperwork involved, I thought about the connection between child and father, which I was witnessing on the panel. Suddenly, the thought of my being a father someday did not feel so remote. If these other single parents did it, why couldn't I? They were not superhumans. I left the workshop feeling empowered.

After the single-parent adoption seminar, I started talking to a select group of family and friends. I say "select" because I didn't want to tell everyone. If I changed my mind, what would I say to them later? Everyone I told was supportive, but many asked some hard questions: "Who will take care of the baby during the day?" "How old will you be when he enters college?" "Are you sure you want a boy? Why not a girl?" "How will you handle the gay issue?" My friend who had adopted told me that although extremely rewarding, it is difficult for him and his partner to raise a child and he couldn't imagine doing it alone. He also called adopting as a single parent "a crazy thing to do." At first, I thought this an unfair judgment, but the more I thought about it, the more it became a slogan for me: Yeah, it is a crazy thing to do, but crazy is not necessarily bad.

My family has been very supportive of my adoptions, especially my mother. Through my sister, I heard about something my mother did of which I am very proud. She and my sister and her two boys were at a Unitarian Church service one Sunday where a lesbian couple was showing off their new baby girl they had adopted from China. My mother, who was seventy-five at the time, went right up to them and said, "My son is gay and is adopting a baby boy!" I am proud of her because she was not embarrassed to say, "My son is gay." She is outwardly proud of me for who I am and that I am taking steps to realize my dreams. When I told her I was writing a book, she commented, "The right-wing Christians are not going to march in front of your house, are they?" She is the cutest, sweetest mom any guy could want. From her, I have received immeasurable strength.

As I shared my adoption plans with friends and family, I realized that, although their opinions and support were helpful, the decision was mine and mine alone. I would be the dad. I would be responsible for another human being for the next twenty years and beyond. I knew I had a great desire to be a parent, and I knew I could do it logistically and financially. Still unanswered, however, was whether I could handle it emotionally on a day-to-day basis. How do straight dads handle it emotionally? Do they even think about that? How do you gain the patience needed to raise a child? At the time, this was all speculation, but I believed I would be able to handle what was put before me at any time. I thought about my struggle for my identity as a gay man. When I tapped into that process, I realized that I'd climbed hills as steep as this before and it had all come together over time. This resource was invaluable to me and is one that I could count on to help me through the times when I was doubtful about being a father. I believe gay men and lesbians sometimes forget how much stronger they are because of their struggle to become themselves.

Another big unknown for me while I was making the decision to adopt was the question of whether being a single dad would prevent me from having another long-term relationship. The parameters for dating would be the same as if I were a divorced or widowed mom. I thought about the movie *Alice Doesn't Live Here Anymore* (1974)—a courageous single mom makes it work and provides for her son, but dating is not easy for her. Would that be my story too? Dating someone with a baby or child is uncharted territory for gay men. Would it make me less attractive or provide some extra appeal? Would the guys I date think they were not getting enough attention? As I pondered all of this, I decided that, although a great concern for me, it was not enough to stop me from going forward with adopting.

I decided to have a homestudy done. (A homestudy is a document all about the prospective parent, including discipline beliefs, financial circumstances, police clearances, home environment, etc.) I figured that if I did not go through with the adoption, if I changed my mind, I would have lost only the homestudy fee. Once I took this path, however, it was difficult to turn back. Now, it seems that I could interchange the term "homestudy" with "reality check" because that is what it was for me. Many parts of the homestudy stimulate thinking about the issues of parenting. Although a lot of paperwork, I found it a welcome challenge when I considered the possible outcome. Around the same time, I applied to the Immigration and Naturalization Service (INS) to bring a foreign-born child into the United States. (In March 2003, the INS began operating under the Department of Homeland Security as the BCIS, Bureau of Citizenship and Immigration Services.)

A few more months had passed when I saw a two-line message on a Vietnam Adoption Listserv (an Internet bulletin board): "I am trying to find a home for one newborn healthy infant boy. Please contact me if you would like further details." I responded right away, indicating my interest. The sender sent by e-mail more details about the baby and a photo. Then a package arrived with three more photos taken when the baby was about twelve days old. I was then asked to send funds to start the adoption of that baby boy if I was still interested. Two couples were also interested, so time was an issue. To say I was scared during this time does not even slightly capture the feelings of uncertainty, trepidation, and near panic I was experiencing. I felt alone even though my friends and family were supporting my efforts. Then I realized that people do this all the time—that is, they give themselves to another human being for long periods of time, whether in a parental or spousal role. I tried to think ahead forty years to take a look back on this decision, to allow myself to ask, "What is a natural dad going to do for the next twenty years without a child to raise?" Then I thought, here is this child, who is available for me to adopt, albeit sooner than I had expected. I checked some references and sent the money.

That baby boy is now my son Andrew. The daddy in me has finally come out and loves every minute of fatherhood. It is impossible to put in writing how it feels after all of these years to realize my dream. I believe these kinds of events happen in one's life if and when they are supposed to, so this must be what was meant to be. My life feels more complete; I have a purpose to my life and I will leave a legacy. After I came home with Andy, I asked myself, "Did I do this for him or for me?" Honestly, I'd say it seems about equal; I want to be a parent *and* I want to provide a good home for a child. It is a win-win situation. I love being his dad, and from all responses I am getting so far, he loves being my son.

Chapter 2

Sacrifices and Trade-Offs— Kids versus Corvettes

I remember pulling Andy out of the bathtub one night thinking that very few, if any, of my peers must be doing what I'm doing tonight. He was screaming because he had a bad case of diaper rash and the bathwater was not soothing him as I thought it might. Thus, his bath, which is usually a fun time, was painful and short. I washed him very quickly and pulled him out to get ready for bed. As he was screaming, I wondered what all the single gay guys downtown were doing. Maybe they were out for a movie or a drink. It was a nice night, so I imagined there were very few empty tables at the sidewalk restaurants. I dutifully dressed the diaper rash with ointment, which calmed him down quite a bit, then put his pajamas on, and we read a few stories. When he finally went to sleep, I thought again about my peers. I felt a longing for some of the freedom of my former life. I just wanted to be selfish. Then I realized I needed milk for the next morning's breakfast and I had forgotten to get it that evening, but now I couldn't leave the house.

As ominous as that sounds, fatherhood has infinite rewards that certainly outweigh the difficult moments. Even as I imagined my peers while Andy was screaming, I thought, yeah, it would be nice to be out tonight, but this is where I belong. This home, this family, is my life. Now that I have adopted Andy, I freely accept all the sacrifices that go with parenting. I always joke that when you get a baby, you get patience and a video camera—as if they are standard issue. Because I have more patience than I used to, that night after Andy's quick painful bath, I was able to calmly reduce his pain, and mine too. Now I am able to put my sacrifices in perspective. At the end of the day, even on the tough days, I go to bed knowing I am doing *my* thing.

I may have less freedom than I used to, but I am always content with my life and the choices I've made.

What are the sacrifices facing a single parent? Some are emotional, such as loss of your selfishness, and some are practical, such as not being able to go to the 7-Eleven for milk. I didn't ponder extensively the practical sacrifices before I became a parent—I was probably too busy worrying about the emotional part of it. The sacrifices I list are the ones that have affected me. As you can imagine, some of these would be absent in a household with two parents.

I am thankful that I did some traveling before I adopted Andy because traveling with a child is certainly more difficult. For the next few years, our vacations will probably be not too far from home. Car trips are much easier because I can load the car with all the baby stuff I need. Spontaneity was part of my past life. As a dad, I have had to become a planner. I find that I am more comfortable knowing what's around the corner. I am sure that I will become more adventurous as the boys get older. I plan to take them back to Vietnam someday, perhaps to meet their birth mothers, if they are interested.

Every year, in my life before Andy, when the Oscar nominations were announced, I played a little game with myself, hoping that I'd seen all of the Best Picture nominees. This past year, I saw only one of them—and was happy for that. It seems as if not many Oscar contenders come out on video until well after the awards are given, in essence, yesterday's news. For party conversation, this becomes a canyon between you and your childless friends, one of many alterations to your previously single social environment.

When you become a parent, your social landscape changes. What is important to you—or at least what fills your everyday life—is not the same for your friends who don't have kids. I have remained close with a couple of my good friends who aren't parents and have gained quite a few friends who are gay parents. Gay parents like to be around other gay parents, and most of the time they are not talking about *gay* parenting issues, just toilet training, binkies, naps, day care, and preschool—every parent's issues.

Abiding by a strict nap schedule is very important in our house, though it seems to cramp my style. On the weekends, I find myself scheduling social activities or shopping trips around naps. (I have a theory that naps are God's way of transitioning childless adults into parents. The younger the baby, the more naps taken. This allows the parent(s) to get some things done and perhaps steal a nap too.) As the baby gets older, the naps come twice daily, then once a day at about age one and a half or two. By then the parents' routine is so ingrained in their lives that it's all second nature. Had I known that the baby's naps could be so beneficial to the parent, I would not have worried so much about how my life was going to change. Having a strict nap routine and sticking to it also helps in the effort to get the baby to sleep through the night. For Andy, this happened at about six months old, and for Vincent, at about eight months old, which for both was about one month after arriving home from Vietnam.

My television schedule changed drastically as well when I became a parent. I am now easily entertained by kids' shows. It is a little scary how many times I say to the kids, "We've seen this one before." I never thought I would allow the boys to watch as much TV as I do, but it really does help me steal a few moments to cook dinner, do laundry, and so forth. Very often—mostly after dinner—we sit and watch a movie, so that they know I'm interested in what they enjoy. I also like to have time when the TV is off. I do not want them to grow up thinking that they will be entertained constantly by the television. I want them to learn how to entertain themselves.

When I first adopted Andy, I expected the diapers and formula to be expensive. Diapers averaged only twenty cents each and both boys now no longer need formula. I am lucky, too, that they have six boy cousins, so they wear hand-me-downs quite often. Clearly, the big cost is day care. My household is now among those with more money going out than coming in. Then, always in the back of my mind, I worry about saving enough for college. As a step toward planning for it, I've opened a tax-advantaged college savings plan (a 529) that hopefully will help.

As a single parent, you can't nudge your partner or spouse in the middle of the night and mumble it is his turn to go and feed the baby or check the forehead of a feverish toddler. When I adopted Andy, a colleague said, "Welcome to the sleep-deprivation club." Not only am I sometimes up in the middle of the night, but also sleeping in on weekend mornings has become a thing of the past. Andy and Vincent wake up between 6:30 and 7:30 a.m. every day, Saturday and Sunday included. Although the lack of sleep was difficult at first, I've come to enjoy our weekend mornings together. The older they get, the more I enjoy doing things with them, even if it is simply clowning around on the living room floor or watching Saturday morning cartoons. I sleep less now that I have kids, but they are the best reason in the world to wake up every day. As my dad used to say, "I'll sleep when I'm dead."

The most time-consuming part of parenthood for me is food preparation. (I wish that cooking came as naturally to me as being a dad! I guess we are born with only so many talents.) I recall one night when I made minestrone from scratch. Andy didn't eat any of it. I thought he would at least like the pasta pieces, but I was wrong. I don't get upset anymore if I've cooked a big meal and they don't touch it. I just go to the refrigerator and get out a piece of cheese or bologna for them and enjoy my own dinner. Kids under two seem more comfortable grazing all day; for them to eat a lot at one meal is unusual. I try to be creative every once in a while, but it seems that we eat many of the same things repeatedly. Perhaps that is because I know what they will and will not eat. When Andy turned one year old, my pediatrician told me that he should eat whatever I was eating—no more formula. An unvoiced "uh-oh" sounded in my brain. I couldn't rely on the canned nutrition of the formula or the little bottles of baby food anymore; I had to prepare balanced meals for another person. I added a few more meals to my menu, but he still wouldn't eat much. I talked to a few friends who are parents and discovered that all kids this age are picky eaters. I decided to stock my kitchen with foods high in calcium, protein, and calories and not to worry about it. Baggies of graham crackers or cheese turn up in my coat or shirt pockets because I always have snacks on hand when we go out. I realized that they will eat when they are hungry as long as it's available for them. I still think the constant planning for and preparation of food for children is a huge task, but we have adjusted fairly well.

A good parent makes sacrifices. I understood my parents' sacrifices much better when I became a parent. I have a clear memory from the mid-1960s of my father saying something that he may not even remember. I grew up in a large Irish-Catholic family. My dad always drove used Volkswagen buses—the first minivans. My mother would sit in the backseat to control the crowd of kids. I was the oldest boy, so, very often, I sat in the front passenger seat next to my dad. I was about ten or eleven and very aware of the different models and styles of cars on the road. I noticed a shiny new Corvette as it pulled up next to us. I commented on the Corvette to my dad as my brothers gazed at the car through the side window. I asked my dad why we didn't have one of those, knowing full well that we couldn't afford any new car, much less a Corvette. My dad responded that he could have one of those cars, but he'd rather have us kids. After all these years, I still think of that response and how it made me feel. My dad thought that we were more important than anything and, that day, he told us so. Maybe being a natural parent runs in the family. All of my five siblings have children; none of us has a Corvette.

Chapter 3

My Journey to Vietnam

One of the best ways for me to deal with the intense feelings and uncertainties surrounding adoption as a single guy was to write about it while it was happening. I kept a journal on my second trip to Vietnam, when I became Andy's dad and brought him home to the United States. Let's go back to summer 1998.

Tuesday, August 18, 1998

"Today is the first day of the rest of my life" I found myself muttering this morning. That phrase has never had so much significance for me as it does today because, today, I begin my journey to Vietnam to become a father. I am on a plane to Los Angeles where I will board another to Hong Kong, then another the next day to Ho Chi Minh City, where I will be reunited with Andy, my son-to-be.

I barely got three hours of sleep last night—seems like there were 100 last-minute preparations. I was constantly worrying about forgetting something. This time the preparations are for two. I have never had to pack for two before. Trying to think of everything that I will need to care for an infant is a huge challenge. From now on my life will be this way. My boring, sometimes lonely, sometimes self-centered, sometimes exciting freedom will be absent for a while. But somehow, I feel peaceful about it. I know what I am facing in the next year may not be best described as peaceful, but there is a contentment that I possess now that is carrying me through this journey. I woke up this morning knowing that I had an early taxi to catch, to catch a bus to catch a flight. Then I thought, Oh my God, I am leaving the United States today, by myself, to take a baby from his homeland to be my son whom I must take care of always. Then I got in the shower and headed onward.

By myself—that is the phrase that echoes so heavily for me today. Just last night, as I was going to the drugstore to get some last-minute items for my trip, I saw two guys attempting to cross the street. My automatic presumption was that they were partners or boyfriends. The next feeling I had was wondering, What am I doing to my chances of having that sort of innocence again? Well, I am absolutely uncertain about that. While this was the most powerful and difficult issue facing me as I made the decision to adopt, it did not deter me.

I have just turned forty-three, and I am about to become a father of a four-and-one-half-month-old little boy. He and I will be a family. I truly believe in destiny when these huge life events unfold. I must say that as I have been preparing to bring a baby into my life, I haven't been happier in several years. I was in my element when I spent the weekend with him in June, when he was just ten weeks old. The natural dad in me kicked in. I remember thinking then that even if I was a dad for just two days and that was all the parenting I was meant to do, it was wonderful and fulfilling. I cried many times that weekend, tears of joy and also of fear. What an incredible feeling when he stared at me while I was giving him his bottle. It's as if he were saying, "Take care of me," and I was saying, "OK, I will." Until you are there, it is impossible to know how it feels.

Many people my age are parents, but I have an awkward feeling that, in society's view, I am doing something extraordinary with my life. Because I am a gay man, being a father is not necessarily something that was expected of me. But, I do not think what I am doing is extraordinary; it is just part of who I am. I know that I have a need to be a parent and I've found a child that needs a home. It may seem extraordinary to others, but it isn't to me. Society tends to set parameters on how we are supposed to live our lives, and I had to realize that it was OK to go outside those parameters. That said, I still feel isolated and scared. Isolated because there are very few role models out there for gay men who want to be parents. And, I am afraid that my gay friends might not know how to offer support, at least in the beginning.

Thursday, August 20, 1998

I am approaching the Ho Chi Minh City airport now. I will see Andy within hours. I have told so many people of my adoption plans—the most recent was the flight attendant on this plane. Perhaps I just need everyone's approval and encouragement. I need to feel that

I am doing the right thing. I know a year from now I will think, How silly of me to wonder if this was the right decision. I would be dishonest with myself if I didn't admit that even as I approach Ho Chi Minh City today, I have some small doubts. What I am most sure about is that I am physically and financially able to be a parent. I really believe I am capable of caring for an infant through his adulthood. But, do I want to do this? A small part of me is hesitant to give up my freedom—an infant requires so much care and hard work and I am not looking forward to the lack of sleep I've heard so much about. Where I feel most vulnerable is whether or not I'll be able to handle all the issues and problems that arise. I believe that I am a good person who is levelheaded and will hopefully provide Andy with what he needs emotionally, rationally, and intellectually to get through tough times. But what about the teasing he may get in grade school for having a gay dad, or two dads? What about those rebellious teen years when he is discovering his identity? Questions and situations will arise that will be difficult. But, I believe that there will be a rhythm to our lives, which has its basis in love and day-to-day communication. I have decided not to worry about the teen years now—what new father does? Everyone around me says, "You're going to be a great father," so I have to believe them.

After the plane landed, Don, my adoption facilitator, was at the airport to greet me. After we checked into the hotel, we went to his mom's house where I was reunited with Andy. He smiled at me right away so I thought that maybe he remembered me from when I first met him two months ago. However, after spending a few days with him, I found out that he smiles at everyone. He is a charmer. Everywhere we go people are drawn to him and curious about his situation. They say, "Vietnam?" meaning, "Is he Vietnamese?" I smile and say yes. People are constantly asking, "Where is your wife?" I explain that I am single and the girls giggle. They don't understand how a guy could take care of a baby.

I stayed at his foster home for several hours with Don's nieces, Quyen and Bao, who are the caregivers. They are sisters in their early twenties. I watched them care for him (on the advice of my U.S. pediatrician) so that I could imitate them. This might lessen the shock of his transition from their care to mine.

Don is a Vietnamese American. A family in California adopted him at age fourteen after the war ended. His story is sad in many ways but indicative of the strong will of the Vietnamese. He spent over a year on a boat outside the Philippines with thousands of other refugees. After watching his sister drown in a boating accident, which he survived, he waited in the blazing sun with two square feet to sleep on for over a year before he was adopted. Food was delivered by helicopter. He commented to me once that the United States is the most compassionate country in the world. All of the other countries that took the children off his boat wanted the young and healthy ones first. Only the Americans, with assistance from their missions and relief charities, took the older children. Don was very proud of his U.S. citizenship. He has since reconnected with his mother and brother and other relatives in Ho Chi Minh City.

When I returned to the hotel, it was just Andy and I. We were playing—I was trying to make him laugh and at one point I got close to his face. He reached up with his hands and touched my face all over as a blind person might do. It was as if he were really checking me out by seeing and feeling my face. It was one of those moments that seemed to define the beginning of our relationship.

Sunday, August 23, 1998

My first trip to Ho Chi Minh City was just two months ago, but somehow I had forgotten how crazy this city is. It is alive with activity all day and almost all night. The sights, smells, and sounds are plentiful. The architecture is pleasing to the eye and the city is planned well, at least in the main downtown area. The Saigon River winds through the city, where you can see floating restaurants and evidence of a bustling port. There is a constant drone of motorbikes coming and going—like a beehive. Some friends described it as "magical," and I completely concur. Unemployment is very high but is probably not quantified. How can you say that the little nine-year-old girl on the street (who speaks fluent English) selling gum from a placard over her shoulders is unemployed? The Vietnamese people are very friendly and always willing to talk to Americans. There is food on the street corners, which adds to the heat and smell of the city. And, as in any Asian city, the smell of raw fish is part of daily life. Getting across the street is an exercise learned in one day—maybe two or three for the timid. In the main streets, there are two lanes, one for motorbikes and one for cars. Crossing the motorbike lane is harder than the car lane as there are so few cars in Saigon. It is every person for himself and you must always be looking in the direction of the oncoming motorbikes. If they see you, they will avoid you, so you could walk into a crowd of them and get to the other side without anyone running you down or shouting at you. It is defensive driving and defensive crossing. No one here is an angry driver. If there is ever an accident, it is usually at low speeds and therefore only results in scrapes and bruises.

I love this city. I have to keep reminding myself about that as I go through the adoption process. The tasks at hand are fully consuming and taxing, to the point where it is difficult to see and feel all that is around you. I decided to make efforts to enjoy Vietnam and make time for learning about it for Andy's sake. As he gets older, I want to educate him on his culture and share as much of it as I can with him. The more I know, the more I will be able to communicate with him and make him proud of his home country.

Tuesday, August 25, 1998

I am officially a father. The "Giving and Receiving" ceremony took place today and it was very emotional for me. Ceremony is probably not the best description for the event, as there was no pomp or circumstance—only some paperwork for the birth mother, Kim Hoa, and me to sign. She is pretty. Today was the first time I met her. Although she was all smiles, there was some uneasiness about her—you could see her heart breaking just under the surface. In the very beginning of the ceremony, I gave her Andrew to hold and she played with him for the entire ceremony. Thank goodness he was well behaved, but he usually is. I was cautious with her. I wanted to be friendly, but the language barrier was in the way and since we were supposed to be paying attention to the event, there was little or no chance for small talk through a translator. I just smiled a lot and hoped she understood that I recognized the sacrifice she was making. While I was watching her hold him, I was thinking about the extreme emotional bond that must exist between a mother and her child and how difficult it must be for her to let him go. However, I must admit that the most painful emotions swirling around in my heart that day were not about Kim Hoa and her sacrifice, but about the risk that she would change her mind. This consumed me because I had fallen in love with her little boy and I could not bear it if she decided to keep him. We signed all the necessary papers. I went first. Kim Hoa is illiterate and could not print her full name so she was asked to sign the main registry with her fingerprints. I imagine that she was a bit embarrassed because no other fingerprints were on the page. The registry we were signing was a huge book of green ledger sheets where others signed on as new parents and birth mothers signed away rights to their recently born children. I signed and she fingerprinted a couple more documents as Don told me to keep smiling. At one point, the woman who was registering all the paperwork asked me why I wanted to adopt. Through Don's translation, I said to give a good home to a child in need. She then asked, "Why Vietnam?" I had to think about this one for a moment. The real reasons are because the children are younger, the process is faster than other countries and somewhat easier. (But, as I write this, I think this process is anything but easy—especially for the heavy-hearted.) So, I explained that there are many children in Vietnam who are in need of homes and that I have always found the Vietnamese very friendly. After the ceremony, Don told me that during the ceremony the woman asked Kim Hoa, "Your son is so cute, why do you want to give him up? Don't you love your son?" To which she answered, "Yes, of course I love my son, but I want him to have a better life in the United States." I was thankful that I didn't understand Vietnamese so I didn't hear this exchange at the time. I would have been scared that the woman was trying to talk Kim Hoa out of her decision. She did, after all, have that option until the last paper was signed.

The first part of the ceremony took about one hour. The building where it took place was a typical government building that had no air-conditioning, no computers, no flush toilets; dirt and dust were everywhere. It was hot as blazes too. It must have been ninety-five degrees in the shade and very humid. Andy was dressed in an embroidered traditional Vietnamese outfit. He looked very nice, although a little uncomfortable.

When we went outside, Kim Hoa was still holding Andy. We stood around a bit and I was about to cry when she came up and handed Andy to me. It was a very symbolic gesture, as I am sure she intended it to be. She did not look me in my eyes—if she had she might have seen the tears there. Perhaps she was avoiding an emotional situation. I told Don later that this must have been so difficult for her. He told me that this was not as emotional for her as the time she went in front of the "local committee" a few weeks ago. The local committee is a body of military, government, and local community officials who enforce law and order within each province. Hearing about this committee reminds me that this country still has it roots firmly planted in socialism. Apparently, the local committee grilled Kim Hoa on the circumstances of her pregnancy and her decision to place her baby for adoption, even though they were encouraging her to do so. Don said she was a brave woman to do this and that she cried at the end of the hearing. For her, today's ceremony was merely signatures and a chance for her to meet me, which Don said she had been looking forward to.

We had to return to the same office in the afternoon, but Kim Hoa did not. We said our good-byes to Kim Hoa and Don told her that we would try to visit her village before we left for the United States. She seemed happy that she would get to see Andy once more.

Although it was a relatively short ceremony, it was a long and emotional morning. We were hungry, exhausted, and quite wound up, so Don, Andy, and I went to a riverside restaurant to have some Vietnamese lunch. The restaurant was almost empty but had a full staff, so Andy got a lot of attention. We sat out on the patio near the Dong Nai River and the waitresses took Andy because each one wanted to hold him. Don and I ordered beers to celebrate, although that is unusual for me in the middle of the day. There was only one waiter among the crew and I had a feeling that he might be gay. He was quite taken with Andy and held him quite a bit. I thought about this man's situation. He was working in a restaurant in a remote province, about an hour and a half outside Ho Chi Minh City. If he was gay, was he closeted or out? Do they even think in those terms over here? He seemed like a "natural dad" from the way he was with Andy. I realized how lucky I am to be gay in the United States, where being gay is still a struggle, but not nearly as bad as it might be in other countries, especially in the third world. Also, I thought, how lucky I am to realize my dream of becoming a father. Would this man ever have the same opportunity? Perhaps I was speculating a little too much, but pondering this man's situation certainly made me grateful.

After a long lunch, we went back to the government office. The giving and receiving ceremony was finally complete at about 4:30 p.m. on August 25, 1998, except for one minor detail. I did not have my hotel's stamp on my yellow entry slip that is supposed to be in my passport. (This is a stamp that foreigners who come to Vietnam are supposed to get from their hotel, but no one does.) For all practical purposes, Andrew is my son now and we will celebrate August 25 as "Gottcha Day," as other adoptive parents and their children do.

On the way back to Ho Chi Minh City, as we wove through the traffic and constant oncoming vehicles in our lane, I was holding Andy and I told Don, "I can't believe I am a father." I also said that I can't believe in a year or so, I'll be saying to Andy, "It is past your bedtime, little buddy." Don looked out the window in the other direction, and I knew that this brought up emotions for him. It seems that all of us were on the verge of tears that day. I did mine in private at the hotel later that night, at 4:00 a.m., while Andy was sleeping. I just broke down and cried. It was my "postpartum depression," or as close to it as I got. My tears were a result of worrying that something could still go wrong and the overwhelming feeling that I am now responsible for raising a child. I cried a flood of tears. I just couldn't stop.

During the twenty-four-hour period following the Giving and Receiving ceremony, I spent about $340 on international phone calls, mostly to the United States. I called the INS office in Washington, and the one in Bangkok. I also called my brother and my sister in Virginia. I was trying to see if I should register the INS paperwork from DC or Bangkok. If I did it from DC, it could save us some time, but as it turns out, they are not as familiar as the Bangkok office is with Vietnam adoptions. Most of the expense was worthless because I didn't accomplish anything on the paperwork front. I did, however, let my brother know that I was officially a dad now and he could therefore come to Vietnam to join me. The plan was for him to come to Vietnam to help me, but not before the Giving and Receiving ceremony took place. I didn't want him to get on a plane until Andy was my son, after having heard stories of adoptions not going through. Also, I was able to tell my sister, Eileen, that I was now a dad, and I cried because she said she was so proud of me. At one point, she heard Andy through the phone and she cried out of happiness for me.

Perhaps my tears that night were also a result of my frustration with the paperwork. The whole process is a seemingly unending stream of difficult paperwork. It is as if we work on one piece per day and the effort for each piece is monumental. Such as driving one and one-half hours each way to the province, in the extreme heat, waiting for a bureaucrat to come back from a long lunch, only to be told that we need a certain stamp from a certain agency or hotel or doctor, thus having to return the next day. On top of all of this, my new infant son was suffering in the heat with a bad case of diarrhea. When I started the adoption process, I was able to get all of the paperwork completed for my homestudy and for the Vietnam Dossier with pretty good timing. Paperwork and deadlines are what I do for a living, so it was not that foreign to me. But as I sit here in Ho Chi Minh City for the eighth day, I am reminded about Murphy's Law—What can go wrong, will go wrong. The bureaucracy in Vietnam is unbelievable. It seems that the government is antiquated and has no revenue from taxation because no one pays taxes even though taxes are due. No tax revenue means no changes in the old systems, no computers, no air-conditioning, etc. It makes you wonder when and if it will ever get better.

Wednesday, August 26, 1998

Today was the worst day I have had in Vietnam so far. My stomach was in knots after witnessing what I did shortly after 1:00 p.m. That is when we were to meet with the woman who conducted the Giving and Receiving ceremony to show her the hotel stamp on my arrival card. It was ninety-five degrees that morning, so I am sure it was over 100 by the time we arrived. I was holding Andy the whole time because there was no clean place to put him down. We arrived on time, but the woman was not there. She arrived at 1:30 p.m. and shortly thereafter came a French couple carrying a baby who was about three months old. I tried to talk to them but as soon as I did, I could tell something was wrong. They butted in front of us to speak to the woman we were waiting to see, but we did not protest. Any such outbreak could jeopardize our task. Don overheard some of the conversations and told me that something was wrong with their paperwork. Then I saw the adopting mother break down in tears, and Don told me that their case was rejected due to a baby-selling scandal. The adopting father then cried, as did their adoption facilitator. Don said that someone turned them in. The adopting parents or the agency may not have been guilty of anything. I told Don not to tell me anymore right then because I was too upset. To watch them cry was very painful for me, so I took Andy and walked around outside as much as I could while trying to avoid the sun. I felt as if I had witnessed them getting the news that someone had just died. They were carrying this baby boy, so I presumed that they had been caring for him at their hotel like I had been caring for Andy. To see them watch their whole process fall apart in one moment was devastating because I am in the same process—although further along. It reminded me of the tremendous vulnerability of this adventure. It truly is a leap of faith. I wish the best for them. I hope they are able to clear this up and proceed, but it seems doubtful. Perhaps they will have to start over. I really wish I had not witnessed this today. It left me feeling insecure about my ability to be a father. To witness their loss shattered some of my confidence, which I know should not be connected, but it just is. I feel better now as I write this, but I will never forget witnessing their pain. I just want to take Andy and go home! Thank God my brother Dennis is coming and I will have his support through the rest of the maze, then also on the journey home.

On the way back to the hotel, Don shared with me more about the baby-selling scandal. Apparently, there were women who were being paid to pose as birth mothers who would relinquish rights to the babies being put up for adoption. In Vietnam, unless a baby is in an orphanage (and is thus a ward of the state), a birth mother must give up her baby freely. Any judge officiating over a direct adoption (direct—meaning from the birth mother directly to the adopting parent) would question the origin of the child if it was suspected or discovered that the birth mother was an impostor. In such a case, the baby could have been abandoned, but if it wasn't, the judges might suspect it was stolen or purchased. Thus, for direct adoptions they were only approving airtight cases where the local committee knew the birth mother, saw her during her pregnancy, and knew that she is freely giving up her child. Andy's case was that way and Don has assured me that we had no such problems. I still had some fear around this issue after watching the French couple being turned away.

Don also shared with me how he got connected to Andy. His brother knew someone who knew someone at the hospital where Kim Hoa gave birth to Andy. When she was pregnant, she was considering her options. The hospital staff encouraged her to give the baby up for adoption based on her worries about providing for him. She is single and a farm worker and could not take time off to raise a child. Don said she was content with her decision, which was apparent during the Giving and Receiving ceremony.

Saturday, August 29, 1998

My brother Dennis arrived in Ho Chi Minh City this morning. The sight of him exiting the Ho Chi Minh City airport through the massive crowd awaiting new arrivals is etched in my mind. I left Andy at Don's mom's house because the airport and arrival waiting area, which is all outdoors, is no place for an infant. I hugged Dennis and said, "Welcome to Saigon," like I was a seasoned resident. (I felt like a resident after just ten days because of the way the culture sucks you in.) He said when he thought about his vacation plans earlier this year, he never thought in his wildest dreams that he would spend two weeks in Vietnam. I was extremely happy to see him. I needed his advice, companionship, and his listening ear as I aired out my frustrations with the adoption process thus far. With Dennis there, I didn't feel as scared and vulnerable. Vietnam, all of the sudden, did not feel quite so foreign as it did the day before.

We went back to the hotel. We knew that Andy would be napping at Don's mom's so we had a few hours before we picked him up. We decided to go to the Presidential Palace, which was the home of the South Vietnamese president before Saigon fell to the North in April 1975. It is now officially called the Reunification Palace. We each took a "cyclo," which is a three-wheeled bicycle with a seat on the front. It is a tourist thing to do. We failed to negotiate the price of a ride to the Presidential Palace, so when we arrived there, we were asked for about $40. We knew this was way too much, so after much broken-English bickering and Vietnamese Dong thrown back at us by the drivers, we ended up paying $10 to each driver. Then we found out the palace was closed for lunch for an hour. We walked to a cyber-café and tried to send some e-mails and have some spring rolls, but soon after we got settled the electricity gave out. Dennis noticed that the Coke cans had the old-style pull-off rings that used to be around in the United States in the 1970s. Dennis is a father of twins and is Mr. Safety.

The cost to get in the palace for Westerners was US $5.00. (There is a smaller fee for locals.) The Vietnamese have strict laws on using currencies other than their Dong except in government-run tourism spots. I found it ironic that they take only U.S. dollars and then say a lot of bad things about Americans when you get inside. The palace was a huge, somewhat cold building with many rooms for many purposes. There was an extensive maze of "war rooms" underground. This building was one of the major command centers for the South Vietnamese Army. The tour guide would refer to the war as the "American war." They called it that because they felt that the American presence prolonged and escalated the Vietnam War. My own impression after I was in Ho Chi Minh City for a short period is that they were probably right. There was quite a bit of anti-American sentiment in the tone of these tour guides and other guides that we encountered, but it did not carry over to the general population. Most of the Vietnamese welcomed us with open arms. We had to remind ourselves that the communist government paid the tour guides and probably told them what to say and what not to say. Outside the palace, on the grounds near the front gate, was a tank on display. It was the famous one that stormed the gate on April 30, 1975, causing the surrender of the South Vietnamese president. The war, we discovered, was the mainstay of Vietnam's tourism industry. Although morbid and depressing, it is what they want to show the world and it is what the tourists want to see.

We then went back to the hotel where Don was waiting with Andy. Dennis met Andy outside the elevators on the nineteenth floor. I felt so proud to introduce my new son to his new uncle. We spent the next few days touring and shopping. We always took Andy in the Snuggli (a front-loading baby carrier) because it was the best way to get around and bond with him at the same time.

Monday, September 1, 1998

This morning, we left Andy at Don's mom's house again and took a day trip to Chu-Chi, which is an underground city that the North Vietnamese built about an hour outside Ho Chi Minh City. They were very proud of this man-made marvel so they made it another showpiece of the American war. It was a four-level maze of tunnels made from carving dirt and removing it. They had 6,000 people living in these tunnels at one time. Everyone had a job to do. They had medical and dining facilities and a command center with maps pinned to the dirt walls. The United States knew about the Chu-Chi tunnels and tried to bomb it over and over. There is evidence of this as you walk around aboveground—the giant craters where the bombs fell are labeled B-52, etc. The structure of the tunnels was strong enough to withstand the onslaught and was not destroyed. We went down one level and it was so tight through the tunnels that you could not even crawl on your hands and feet. You could only crouch down, shuffle your feet, and keep your shoulders inward as much as possible. The dirt on the sides of the tunnel stuck to us because our shirts were wet with sweat. The tour guides asked if we'd like to go down another level or two and we quickly declined. At the end of the tour was a gift shop with, among other things, knockoff Zippo lighters with American GIs' names engraved on them.

Tuesday, September 2, 1998

Today, we went to the village where Andy was born to visit his birth mom, Kim Hoa, and her family. I rented the hotel's Ford mini-van for the entire morning. I felt that it would be safer than a taxi van that may or may not have seat belts. Also, I thought the hotel drivers would likely be better-caliber drivers than the standard taxi drivers. We had no way to tell Kim Hoa that we were coming that day. The weather was showing promise of another humid, 100-degree day. With Don and one of his staff who knew where the village was, we set out early to Dong Nai. We stopped along the way to pick up some food to present to Kim Hoa and her family. We bought bread, rice, vegetables, fruit, and two rotisserie-style chickens (at least I think they were chickens—they usually leave the heads on so that you know it is not a cat). The main road was full of motorbikes, pedestrians, goats, chickens, and stray dogs. Other drivers, including huge old trucks, are constantly going left of center to avoid people and animals on the side of the road. It was extremely dangerous and I just prayed that we'd arrive safely. And, of course, there are no infant car seats. I kept telling the driver to drive slowly and carefully. Time was not crucial—we had all day to make this visit.

At first, we could not find their village because we took the wrong road off the main highway. After a few more tries, we finally found the road that would take us to her village. We traveled a long way down a dirt road, leaving a dusty trail behind us. The people on this road obviously had not seen very many shiny minivans before, so we drew a lot of stares as we went by. I filmed part of our journey so I'd have it to show Andy someday. We finally found the area near where Kim Hoa lived and we parked the car. I gave Dennis the video camera and we opened the car doors. Within minutes about ten or fifteen people surrounded the van, including Kim Hoa, who came running with excitement. There was a lot of excited Vietnamese chatter going on but we spoke only with our smiles. We would have to wait until we sat down to translate a dialogue. I immediately handed Andy to Kim Hoa and she was thrilled to see him. She handed him to whom I presumed was her mother, who proceeded to make a big fuss over him. Other than Kim Hoa, who saw him at the Giving and Receiving ceremony, Andy's family had not seen him since he was about six weeks old. Kim Hoa helped with our packages. I looked around and Andy had been whisked off into the brush. I calmly asked Dennis, "Where do you suppose they've gone with my son?" Kim Hoa then escorted us down a dirt path into the shady woods. A couple hundred feet into the woods, as we passed a few wandering stray chickens, we came upon a wooden shack with a corrugated metal roof. Next to it was a small straw house. This was home for their entire family. A crowd of children was growing behind us. Word that the Americans were here must have spread fast in the village. Dennis was videotaping the entire time and I told him to "just keep it going." Although Andy had disappeared down a different path than the one we took, we were reunited with him at Kim Hoa's house. His grandmother was passing him around to his great-grandmother and aunts. There were no adult males in the house. There was quite a lot of exciting conversation and laughter. We were amazed at the whole scene and, again, my emotions were near the surface. They asked about us—who is older and who is taller. They said, for brothers, we really didn't look alike. Kim Hoa presented me with an embroidered cloth that had Andy's Vietnamese name, birth date, and his mother's full name and his province of birth. She also gave me a letter that she asked someone to write for her. It was in Vietnamese, so I'd have to have it translated later. We sat on plastic stools and exchanged a few pleasantries through Don, our expert translator. Their home was one large room with several flat wooden beds where three or four family members would sleep. There was one fluorescent light in the middle of the room. I was surprised to see electricity out this far. We didn't stay too long, mostly because of the language barrier. It certainly takes the spontaneity out of everyday conversation.

    Don suggested that we make this trip, and I felt that we really should to pay our respects to Kim Hoa. Now, as I look back on it, I realized that the visit was all about her. We did not have to go at all, but we did to give her some comfort that we cared enough to recognize the sacrifice she has made. I hope that she takes our visit as a symbolic gesture of how I will raise her son. I wanted her to know that I am a person who keeps his word. She will know very little about me, but, hopefully, she will remember the day we came to her village.

When I returned to Washington, DC, I had the letter translated by two Vietnamese Americans. I was told by Don to have it done twice because the Vietnamese language is often spoken in phrases and word-to-word translation is not always possible. Some of the phrases will translate differently for different readers. The letter is a beautiful note that I am able to share with Andy someday. I realized that if we had not gone to the village that day, she would have not been able to give it to me. Not only do I have photos and video of the village Andy would have grown up in if she had decided to keep him, but I also have this wonderful letter that explains to him the basis of her decision. These things are huge references for me as Andy questions his identity and origins. When I chose Vietnam as the country I wanted to adopt from, I didn't realize that I would meet his birth mother or see her home, or get a letter from her. In Russia and China, which are two of the countries I was pondering, almost all of the children are abandoned. There is very little frame of reference of where your child came from. I have a few more tools to field questions that Andy will most assuredly ask.

After visiting Kim Hoa and her family, I now know that if she had chosen to keep him, he would have had no less love in his family and village as he will have with me and my family and friends. As I raise him, I'll try to explain that to him. The only difference between here and there is that, in the United States, he will have more opportunity.

The letter she wrote to me makes it clear that she is happy that Andy will have a dad, which, as she says, he was born without. Here is the letter she wrote to me:

Dear Mr. Kevin

My name is Trung Phi Kim Hoa, currently residing at Hamlet IV, township of Tham An, Long Thanh County, Province of Dong Nai.

In recent months, with Mr. Don's help, I learned that you would be the adoptive father of my baby Trung Van Phuong. I have these few words to express my gratitude and to explain my and my son's situation.

Because of poverty, I am resigned to sever my parental links, for what mother could bear giving up her child without breaking to pieces inside? Because his ill-fated life started out without the man who made him and because as a single mother I cannot afford to raise him, I have to give him up. Now, since you will adopt him, he will escape a life of want and wandering. When he grows up, he will forever be grateful and loyal to the benefactor who has raised him. He is to grow by your side. I dearly wish that you will provide for him and attend to his every need. Please don't ever abandon him, but show him a father's love he lost at birth. That's all that his mother would ask of you. As long as he is happy, I will be indebted to you for the rest of my life.

These are words from a mother who is about to part with her child forever. If I have said anything to displease you, please forgive me. Once more, Mr. Kevin, please accept my most grateful thanks.

Yours truly,
Trung Phi Kim Hoa

Chapter 4

Being a Gay Dad

STUDY BY GILLIAN DUNNE

Are gay dads good dads? Some research indicates that we are. A study released in 2001 suggests that gay men who are planning to become fathers often give it much more thought than their heterosexual peers.* The author of the study is Gillian Dunne, a senior researcher for the London School of Economics Gender Institute. She noted that "the implications of gay men becoming fathers and constructing parenting identities and practices beyond the confines of heterosexuality are profound" (1.2). Looking back at our parents' generation, when birth control was not as widely used as it is today, men might not have given fatherhood much thought. Today, however, many fathers and mothers discuss what it means to become parents and how they will manage their families.

The study by Dunne demonstrates what I see all gay men do before they become fathers. They think deeply about it and prepare themselves for it to the point that when they do become fathers, they are extraordinarily committed. I have facilitated two discussion groups for gay men considering parenthood (Maybe Baby groups—as they were affectionately called), and I have seen how gay men approach the prospect of parenthood. First is an entitlement issue. As I look back, I remember going through this too. It seems that gay men don't feel entitled to become fathers because they are gay. As it is not biologically possible for them to have a baby with their partners or by themselves, they have to find a way to rationalize their fatherhood within another context. Once they get over the entitlement hurdle,

---

*Dunne, G. A. (2001). "The Lady Vanishes? Reflections on the Experiences of Married and Divorced Gay Fathers," *Sociological Research Online, 6*(3) (November) pp. 1-17, <http://www.socresonline.org.uk/6/3/dunne.html>.

they look to other gay men who are parents as examples and soon realize that maybe they can also be a dad. What being a dad means to each of them is unique, but the common thread for all of these men is deep soul-searching. Part of that may be their concern for the child and what he or she will face growing up, but I am convinced that most of all, because it is so unusual for gay men to become parents, they need to justify it for themselves. Going through this process, and overcoming whatever else they may have to work through, makes them better prepared to be a dad than before they started thinking about it seriously. I don't know whether this makes them great dads, but it would certainly make them more resolved to follow their dreams in a mature and well-thought-out manner. Also, many gay men are older when they become fathers, which might mean that they have more patience, an invaluable asset in parenthood. This is certainly true for me. For nontraditional fathers, choosing fatherhood creates much trepidation, then resolve, and finally pride.

Dunne studied 100 gay fathers and fathers-to-be. She described some of her respondents as "exceptionally active caregivers—with some having put their caregiving responsibilities before career advancement" (4.19). Gay men who overcome the obstacles and opt into fatherhood are more likely to be actively involved in routine child care than other fathers. Because gay men have gone through the coming-out process, they have challenged typical gender roles. This can be beneficial when faced with day-to-day child-rearing duties commonly fulfilled by women. Also, most gay men were brought up in families where they were pushed in ways that weren't right for them, and, therefore, they want to bring up their children to be themselves. Dunne noted:

> Just as the mainstream has much to learn from gay men's experience of parenting, so too does the wider gay community. Gay communities are on the brink of a major transformation as a result of the "gayby boom," and expanding opportunities for fathers to "come out." The greater visibility of gay fathers is likely to enable other gay men to realize that fatherhood is not ruled out for them. (5.2)

In Great Britain, where the study was released, according to Dunne about 50 percent of divorced fathers lose contact with their children within a year of divorce. The participants in Dunne's study who are divorced gay dads, however, were still actively involved in their children's lives; many were actively coparenting or were main caretakers. This, Dunne noted, "is very unusual."

What will we, as gay parents, be subjecting our children to when they (and their peers) become aware that their fathers are different? These issues and the answers to them are pondered by gay dads but are practically far off at the time of adopting a baby or toddler. Certainly, having our children interact with kids of other gay parents will help immensely, but that is not always an option, especially in rural areas. I believe the "thinking deeply" that we all go through before we adopt will help us resolve issues of shame if they ever arise. I also believe that when our children become young adults, they will see their open and honest upbringing as a gift. Many of their peers who are from traditional nuclear families will not have had this gift. If troubles surface along the way, our kids will be stronger as a result. Their identity will reflect their struggle and their strength. And we, knowingly or unknowingly, will pass on to them what we have gained from our struggles.

So, what does it mean to be a father? I find it difficult to explain in writing. Someone once asked me, "How can you explain what chocolate tastes like to someone who has never tasted it?" The same can be asked about fatherhood. Every parent with whom I've spoken about this agrees with me—it is a feeling like no other. I am a father. I may not be able to explain what it means, but I say this with more pride than I have for any other accomplishment.

When you are a dad, it seems as if suddenly you are a member of the "Dad Club." There is no such club (that I know of), but you will find that other dads (and moms) love to talk about their kids and knowing that you are a dad allows them to do so. Colleagues and people that you meet for the first time who have children will open up more easily because they can talk about their kids. For example, I was at a large, all-day meeting for work a while ago and two of the three speakers opened with remarks about their children. Obviously, talking about their kids is common ground with much of the audience and a safe way for them to allow the group to get to know them personally before they launch into their presentation.

Being a gay guy who has not hidden his sexuality to any great degree over the years, it is sometimes shocking for others to find out that I am a dad. Many of my colleagues probably always knew I was gay but never spoke about it to me. So when they find out I am a father, their curiosity is piqued but they are polite. You can see that look in their eyes, as if they are whispering to themselves, "Wait a minute, I thought he was a gay guy." After mentioning Andy to a board member once in passing, I was asked, "You've made me curious. What is your situation?"

For some, fatherhood is basic, a given. It is easy to see the fathering instinct in other men whether or not they are dads. Probably many natural dads never get the opportunity to become fathers, for a variety of reasons, only one of which might be being gay. Now, however, gay men are increasingly realizing that they, too, can expand their families and contribute to society by raising and loving children.

TESTIMONIALS

I asked a few of my friends to share their stories of how they came to adopt. What did they go through emotionally before starting their paperwork? What does fatherhood mean to them? Four such anecdotes follow.

I, John, a single gay man, adopted twin boys, Joshua and Jonathan

I think I had just always assumed that I would be a dad. Especially since I came out a little late and had heterosexual relationships and a marriage, I never thought I wouldn't be a father until my thirties. Also, since my parents took in two foster children when I was a young adult, I had a hand in rearing them and remember distinctly the paternal "instincts" that were aroused. Although I have never cared a lot about progeny, the desire to see and assist the development of children to becoming successful adults seems to me like one of life's greatest ambitions.

I was sitting on the beach the summer I was forty years old, contemplating the apparent failure of yet another attempt at a relationship, and decided that if I was ever going to have a family, partner or no partner, I had better get started before it became too late and I became too old. That, in and of itself, was an emotional process because my parents were a little older than the norm, for which I resented them in high school. I always felt that I was too young when my father died, which, given family history, is something I could be setting my boys up for, unless medical technology advances will allow me to defy the family propensity for heart disease.

I also wondered what becoming a single dad would do to my chance of ever finding a romantic relationship and decided that I just couldn't care anymore. Realistically, I began to question why I thought I wanted a partner anyway, since they can be so much trouble! The irony is that after resolving that issue, I have been very satisfied with my dating.

My reservations largely centered on financial issues. Could I make enough money to support a family by myself? And could I do it without working so many hours that I would never see my family? The two seemed contradictory. Then how would I afford preschool or private schools? The list went on. . . . I think I was blind to some other things, such as travel and socializing. I thought I could do whatever I wanted and just include the babies. That was shortsighted, but I still attempt to do so.

When I walk into the babies' line of vision and they smile when our eyes meet, that says it all: they count on me for safety, security, survival, comfort, love, and, ultimately, identity (Maslow's entire hierarchy of needs). That is what being a father means to me.

I, Philip, with my partner Gregg, adopted a little girl, Elizabeth

After adopting Elizabeth, we mostly got caught up in raising her and then the heartache of all her health issues, lengthy stays in the hospital, etc. Even though it has all really been worthwhile and mostly fun despite all of the above, I guess I forgot to take the time to think of some of the deeper implications.

To begin, it took me a long time to really accept myself as gay. I came out to my family at nineteen but coasted in both the gay and the straight world, was a stud of sorts, and thought I might settle down and get married and raise kids eventually. I should have known that was a load of bull but was deluding myself and not delving too much into things. I was twenty-seven, living in Mexico, and had both a boyfriend and a girlfriend when it dawned on me that the boyfriend was who I loved, gay was who I was, and that was that. I came out to whatever corners of the straight world still weren't aware of my proclivities and settled into my gay happy-ever-after. Kids weren't in the picture. Part of coming out, as far as I knew, was that you couldn't have kids. But if gay was who I was, then I was resigned to all that went with it (or in this case, didn't). I eventually moved to the United States. I still had lots of straight friends and thankfully always disliked the part of gay life where sex is everything: you dress for sex, go out for sex, work out for sex, and generally arrange your life around it. As time went on, I was becoming more and more aware that men were adopting. I paid attention to such stories. I suspected this was something I'd be interested in. I didn't really have time to focus on it because I was busy running around, but it was in the back of my mind. When I met Gregg I guess I was ready. I'd done the gay scene, but, increasingly, I started to understand the limitations therein, and I was ready to listen to the father in me. Fatherhood of course means responsibility, settling down, thinking of the future and even old age (grandchildren!), worrying about somebody else, and none of this is possible to the kings of the dance floor out there. So I guess I had to outgrow that phase of my life to really see that all along there was another sort of man right there: a father. Adopting was my idea, not Gregg's. I was ready and had found a partner who would go along with the plan, and here we are. Short version of my stream of consciousness: I probably had always wanted to raise kids; it just took me a while to come to grips with the father in me.

I, David, with my partner, Seth, adopted a baby girl, Emma

For Seth and me there was no doubt that we both wanted to have children. The issues for us were centered around the right timing and whether it was selfish of us to want to have children. On the timing issue we had concerns about finances and the logistics of raising children and working. We ultimately concluded that there really is no perfect time to have kids. You never have enough money and your career is never at just the right point. We thought much more seriously about whether it is selfish for two gay men to adopt children given this country's socially conservative perspective. Having both been teased during middle school because some thought we were gay, Seth and I were very sensitive to the ridicule that children who are in any way different can endure. Our "Maybe Baby" group really helped us work through this issue. We first came to understand that most every child is different in some way and will face some teasing for that difference. Our Maybe Baby group convinced us that the way to deal with the inevitable teasing over the fact that our child (hopefully children) has two dads is to give the child as much pride and self-confidence as possible. As for society's reaction to our nontraditional family, Seth and I concluded that we could not let the bigotry of others determine the shape of our family and lives. There remains a lot of hatred toward gay people, but we realized that if we let that hatred stop us from adopting, then the hate would have won, and that was not acceptable to us. These conclusions were not easily reached and were the result of months of thinking, discussion, and reading, but now that we have our daughter, I have no doubt that we made the right decision. Maybe it is just the world that Seth and I have created for ourselves, but the reaction we have received to our family has been uniformly positive. Our friends, work colleagues, neighbors, and family have been wonderful. Those who don't approve have been silent. This reaction to our adoption serves as a reminder that the world continues to be more accepting of gay people and our right to lead our lives as we see fit. Hopefully by the time Emma is in middle school, the concerns that Seth and I agonized over will be a distant memory.

I, John, with my partner, Paul, adopted a son, Joseph

Our decision to go ahead with adopting came after a fairly torturous journey, at least from my end. Paul was gung ho about this for the past five or six years. I, on the other hand, was definitely not at that stage until this past year.

Though I think almost any adoptive parent goes into parenting with a much more thought-out and prepared view of what he or she is doing than most natural parents, I think gay parents have an added cultural impediment that makes the decision even more serious and active (as opposed to passive). Just having to go through a homestudy makes you take stock of the serious issues of parenting that many natural parents may not consider until it's too late. In addition, the sometimes torturous adoption process itself really brings things home. I'm sure many fathers today take a more active role in pregnancy, etc., but it's still not the same as going through what many of us have endured.

If there is trouble in the adoption process, like we experienced, you soon find out that the legal process actively discriminates against gay people. We were lucky that our families and our agency were very gay friendly—even progay. But for every good experience, there was one like the awful interview with the INS official in which he barely disguised his disgust once he confirmed in his mind that I was a gay man adopting. While anyone embarking on adoption becomes prepared for hurdles like that, a gay parent encounters a lot more of them, and thus I think develops a resolve even greater than an average parent.

Although I don't think anyone would accuse me of living the stereotypical "wild" gay lifestyle, I'll admit that I did (and do) enjoy the freedoms that being a gay man makes possible. Plus, without the societal trappings of marriage and family, much of the past fifteen years has been spent with little or no preconception that children were inevitable. In fact, I had always thought of myself as a bit too cerebral for children and was convinced that I would not be good with them. As with a lot of gay men, I think I also became determined to overcompensate for my own lack of self-esteem by "excelling," especially in terms of career. For most of the 1990s, I was probably overly obsessed with my rapidly rising career track, and the near constant uncertainty that resulted. Reaching a point of stability, of "getting there," was quite an obsession at times, despite the fact that I really had all I could have wanted with Paul. Even though I knew Paul desperately wanted a child, I was absolutely convinced that I was incapable of being a dad, given all the job and family pressures in my life.

Needless to say, this also led to a lot of friction in our relationship, and it was increasingly clubbed into my head that this decision I was essentially forcing on Paul was going to continue to have serious repercussions as time went on.

Again, while I'm sure any parent, natural or adoptive, reaches a point where becoming a parent is all-consuming, as a gay man, it was very difficult for me both to realize the richness parenting could bring to my life and to place other priorities common to gay life on a lower rack. In 1999, after a pretty dreadful year at work, where I reached the pinnacle of positions at my association and found it to be unbearably political, I really had a wake-up call about what was important in my life and where I should really be putting my energy. Quitting my "career-track" job for something smaller (and less lucrative by far) and more of what I really wanted to be doing was the first step in re-prioritizing. That made it possible in my mind to think of parenting as something that was not only doable but also potentially much more satisfying than so many other options that are possible for a gay man.

I relate this story to a lot of people, not just potential parents, but even more to people agonizing over career and "success," etc., because it really is an amazingly liberating feeling to get to the point where the important things in life become clear and you can put the lesser things in their proper perspective. I agree that it is even more difficult, and accordingly more life changing, for gay men to reach such a point because there are so many cultural stereotypes for a "proper" gay lifestyle, and such a lack of expectations for enriching parts of life, such as being a parent, among other things. One often reads about people reaching a "turning point" in their lives (usually fictional people!), but I can vouch that such things do indeed happen and I look back on it as something that has allowed me to make the most life-changing decisions without regret and open a whole new set of possibilities that the stereotypes don't envision. This makes me think of the incredibly satisfying and intimate relationships I've developed with other gay men, as gay men, throughout the adoption process, that have nothing to do with sex or any other gay stereotype. I don't know if I would have thought in these terms a few years ago.

Ironically, career opportunities that Paul had in early 2000 made it clear to me that we also had the opportunity to start a family, and it made me think a lot about what was really important in not only my life but our lives. While moving to the Midwest was not something I looked forward to, it really was much less that and more the fact that the better alternative that would fulfill Paul, fulfill me, and enrich our relationship was to start a family, regardless of what job or what city we ended up in.

So I think "soul-searching" in my experience is a huge understatement. It literally took me years to come to terms with what I was capable of and what would give real meaning to my life and my relationship. In retrospect, I think this worked to my advantage, since I really couldn't have become a good father in the mind-set I had a few years ago, and it took a lot of active thinking and self-reflection in the past two years to feel that I was both ready and able to share my life with a little boy who would become our son.

And, as an added bonus, the whole adoption experience—even as we encountered problems bringing Joseph into the country—has reinforced in my mind that being gay and being a father can not only be complementary, but also actually have tremendous advantages. I think precisely because the societal expectations are not there, the level of support I've received from family, co-workers, and straight friends has been even greater than if I were straight, almost as if they feel they need to provide greater support because they know the cultural supports are not necessarily there.

Also, the circle of other gay parents that I've inevitably met in the process has been truly dumbfounding to me. Our experience with the INS and others has left me so cynical and untrusting that I am continually astounded by the sheer number of truly wonderful gay men and lesbians that have renewed my faith in the goodness of people. Just seeing the incredible level of caring that they show to their children, and to one another's children (even those that aren't here yet!) and to one another as parents, blows me away. Having the support of these guys throughout this whole process was indispensable. It's been truly inspirational to see their level of commitment in a way that leaves no doubt whatsoever about their dedication to both their own children and their extended gay families. This is even more true since it is not something that one would commonly attribute to gay men and requires much more of an active change in life for a gay man than most parents undergo. I can't conceive of anyone contemplating parenthood who would experience this level of caring without recognizing immediately the emotional richness that this decision can bring to their lives and those around them.

If I had to comment succinctly about the change in mind-set I underwent, I would add that a great part of making this decision was a willingness to take a risk on an unknown prospect that had an infinite potential. Just as quitting a job or entering a relationship entails such a risk, I think it does take a lot of active energy to take a risk that has implications for both the rest of one's life and the life of another person. I would imagine that for many prospective gay parents, a major turning point would be when you realize that taking the step into parenting is worth the risk that your expectations will not always pan out. They inevitably will not pan out all the time—but when they do the rewards can be so much greater than if you never took the risk at all. It does take a lot of work to reach the point where you realize that life is too short not to make a leap of faith.

Chapter 5

The Adoption Process

I am constantly being asked, "How did you do it?" I often respond that, except for a few rough days in Vietnam, the adoption of Andy was easy and I was lucky. It took me a little over five months to complete the adoption. I began my homestudy on March 5 and I became Andy's dad on August 25. For Vincent, I started in January and brought him home in early August. I consider myself to be extremely lucky.

My first adoption was different from most. The major difference was that I found Andy before I signed up with an agency. Most adopting parents sign on with an agency that has a program that is suitable for them (as I did for my adoption of Vincent). Then, they basically get in line with other potential parents and wait for a "referral." A referral is a notice of an available child and usually comes with a photo and a health record.

My adoption of Andy started when I answered a message that I saw on the Vietnam Adoption listserv (an Internet bulletin board with a lot of information about Vietnam adoptions). The message mentioned a healthy infant boy. Not fully trusting such a message, but seeing no harm in responding, I answered it, saying I was interested and was a week or so away from getting my INS approval. I asked Don, the adoption facilitator, which agencies he worked with in the United States and he sent me a couple of names. I called one in Connecticut and eventually signed up with them. I didn't have to engage them—I could have just worked with Don independently—but I wanted some assurances that the funds I was sending to Don would not be completely lost if this adoption fell through. The agency provided me with those assurances and reduced their fee from $3,000 to $1,500 because I had already located a child.

Don had just started his adoption program in Vietnam. Andy was the fourth child he placed out of Vietnam. I spent more than two weeks with him in Saigon. He walked me through all the paperwork piece by piece. At the end of the process, I thought that Don was going to have to reevaluate his time and resources for future adoptions. He had a lot of people working for him in Vietnam, so I presumed that, as his business grew, he would have to assign certain trusted members of his staff to walk potential parents through their paperwork. Or, as they do in China, several adopting parents could go through the process at the same time in a "team."

I often called Don a saint when other people asked about him. He could have left Saigon before we were done, and we probably would have survived just fine, but he stayed with us until we had all of our paperwork and could leave for Bangkok. I remember well the day we left Saigon. In many ways, it felt like the last scenes of the movie *The Year of Living Dangerously* (1982), where outbound flights were few and paperwork had to be flawless. The last thing we needed was Andy's Vietnamese passport. It was Friday and we had just applied for it the day before. If it were not ready on that Friday, we'd have to wait until Monday. We pushed all day, bribing the passport workers with "mooncakes" (i.e., Moon Pies) and cartons of cigarettes. Andy was at the hotel with my brother, Dennis, who was unaware whether we were even close to getting the passport. Finally, after we pushed and begged all day, Andy's passport came through the small hole in the glass window in one of the many booths at the dusty, smelly passport office. Emotionally and symbolically, I compared that passport delivered through that tiny window to a woman giving birth, although I presume not as physically painful. We were finally ready to leave Saigon. I truly loved being in Saigon, and I now look back on that trip as the biggest adventure of my life. But after almost three weeks, I was ready to begin the next phase of the journey. Don and I took a blissful taxi ride back to the hotel where Dennis and Andy were hanging around the lobby. Dennis said, "Did you get it?" He already knew the answer when he saw the smile on my face. High fives abounded. Within two hours, we were at the Saigon airport, boarding a flight to Bangkok, with all the proper paperwork and my new son.

The contrast between these—the paperwork and my son—are obvious. Throughout this whole adoption process, I marveled at how vital but, in the end, meaningless the paperwork is. I no longer have to fill out forms and get them notarized. I do, however, have to fill sippy cups and the bathtub and read stories on a daily basis. The seemingly endless paperwork was my means to this end. It is what I had to do to fulfill my dreams. It seems to be a somewhat colder and more bureaucratic method than the way I became part of my family but, nonetheless, just as emotionally packed.

So, what are the papers needed? It depends on the adoption route you choose, but most international adoptions are similar, aside from slightly different requirements by country. A domestic adoption involves a little less paperwork because you don't have to apply to the BCIS (formerly the INS). If you want to adopt internationally, apply to the BCIS as one of your first steps. The approval from them can take about two months or more. You can find the BCIS application form I-600A on the BCIS Web site <www.bcis.gov> or <www.immigration. gov>.

HOMESTUDY

For every adoption by a U.S. citizen, domestic or international, a homestudy is required, which you might think is a report about your home. Although a homestudy does contain information about your home, it is much more about you and your world. My homestudy was a nine-page notarized document prepared and signed by a social worker. I met with the social worker, Kristie, three times, which was the minimum number of visits. One of the visits must be in your home. Choosing your homestudy social worker is very important, as he or she must be someone you like and with whom you are comfortable being open. I first met Kristie at a meeting I had with a local adoption agency to discuss their China and Russia programs. I told her and the owner of the agency that I was gay and currently single. I figured if they had a problem with either of those they could tell me so and I would look for another agency.

Homestudies are portable; that is, they can be presented to an agency other than the one that prepared it for an adoption program that suits your needs. For example, if you find that the agency that prepared your homestudy does not have a program for the country you are interested in adopting from, you can take your homestudy to one that does. If you are undecided about which country to adopt from, you can get your homestudy done while you research your options. That is what I did, and it offered me flexibility and time. If an agency claims they must do all of the paperwork, including the home-study, you should ask why, and unless it is a legal issue in your state, perhaps you can find another agency. Some agencies charge a nomi-nal fee for reviewing and approving your homestudy if it is prepared by another agency.

The reason that flexibility is so important for single or gay men is that we need to keep our options open. Only a handful of countries al-low single men to adopt and sometimes they close single-parent adoptions or require a certification that you are not gay. Currently, Vietnam, Russia, Guatemala, the Ukraine, and China allow single men to adopt. For BCIS purposes, your homestudy is good for eigh-teen months. This limit used to be one year, but a few years ago, the BCIS increased the time limit to assist families with longer timeta-bles. Some countries limit the validity of a homestudy to less than eighteen months. At the time I adopted Andy, Vietnam required that the homestudy or an update of the homestudy be no older than six months. An update can be done by your social worker for a small fee unless your circumstances have changed, for example, change in resi-dence, health, employer, and so on.

If you are a gay couple, in most cases, one of you will be doing all of the paperwork; that is, the homestudy will be all about you. Your partner will be mentioned as a roommate in your home. In California, Connecticut, Illinois, Massachusetts, New Jersey, New York, Penn-sylvania, Vermont, and Washington, DC, a homestudy may be able to mention both of you as parents (depending on local laws). Since I adopted as a single man, I did not have this issue before me. I did, however, speak to several gay couples who found the homestudy pro-cess a source of frustration for them and their relationship. When I ponder the symbolism of the homestudy being in one of the partner's names, I think about how a lesbian couple handles the issues that arise from one of them being the biological mother and the other not. The issues are probably weightier and perhaps more subconscious but, in some ways, similar. Someday, a gay partner will not have to hide as a "roommate" in a homestudy, but this happens now only in a few states. One of the couples I interviewed said they were not trying to make a political statement, they just wanted a child and would do whatever they had to to get him or her. If you are a gay couple adopt-ing, remember this as you prepare your homestudy. Another couple I spoke to said they have a three-bedroom house; one room will be the baby's room, the other is their room, and the third is a guestroom. They asked me if they should move one of their dressers into the guestroom for the homestudy to make it look as if it is a roommate situation. I am not a homestudy social worker, but I answered that, not only would that be physically difficult, but also emotionally taxing. I do not know if the homestudy social worker would notice or object to their situation, but if he or she did, they should find a new social worker.

Typical homestudies take about six weeks to two months to finish. My homestudy included a paragraph on each of the following subjects (please note that your homestudy may include other sections or may not have some of the sections that mine did; state laws dictate what a homestudy will cover, so there will be differences):

Opening Statement: This description of the document contains licensing information on the agency.

Introduction: This includes the adopting parent's name, address, phone numbers, and date of birth.

Contacts: A description of the three visits with the social worker, with dates, goes here.

Description of Parent: A physical description of the adopting parent is provided here.

Family History: This detailed description of family life includes childhood events as well as parents' and siblings' names and occupations.

Children in the Family: Here you list other children in the home. The second homestudy I did mentions Andy here.

Others in the Household: Here you list other people who live in your home. This is where your partner would be mentioned.

Emotional Stability and Maturity: This description of your emotional state should include how you handle stress. A therapist I visited before I adopted was quoted here.

Compatibility and Marital Satisfaction: This paragraph describes your marriage or divorce, your long-term relationships, or the lack thereof.

Feelings About Children: This should describe how you feel about being a parent.

Parenting Abilities: This paragraph stresses your emotional strengths, including patience, as well as your ability to afford day care. Your attitudes about discipline can also be mentioned here.

Financial Resources: This mentions your annual household income, your financial assets, and your monthly debt. It also details your health insurance. It also may mention your educational background and what college you attended.

Interests and Activities of the Family and Daily Routine: Your hobbies, volunteer work and/or outside activities, and daily schedule are mentioned here.

Religion: Here you describe your religious background and what you plan for your child with respect to religion. Religion is not required by most agencies. If you follow no organized religion, this could be titled "spirituality" or left out altogether.

Attitude of Family Members Toward Adoption: Your extended family's and your attitudes toward raising a child not born to you.

Age of the Prospective Adoptive Parent: This describes your age at the time of the homestudy.

Motivation and Readiness of Applicant: The social worker probably asked why you want to adopt and how you will handle cultural differences. Your answers to those questions go here. This section also describes books you've read on adoption.

Type of Child Desired and Expectations of the Child: This paragraph describes the age and sex of the child you desire and whether you are willing to adopt a special-needs child.

Home and Community and Social Relationships: This section describes your home, including the number of rooms, bathrooms, and whether you have running water and plumbing facilities. This section also provides information about your community resources, such as playgrounds, schools, hospitals, and so forth.

Employment: This describes your current employment, with a reference to your employment verification letter.

Health: This section describes any health problems you may have and a certification from your doctor that you are healthy enough to raise a child.

References: During your homestudy process, you are usually required to obtain three reference letters from people whom you know well. The social worker usually speaks to at least one of them on the telephone and any comments are mentioned in this paragraph.

Preadoption Counseling: This describes any formal adoption or parenting classes you may have taken or seminars attended. In my case, I attended therapy with a therapist who had adopted.

Fire Escape Plan: This describes the entrances and exits of your home in case of fire and presents verification of smoke detectors in your home.

Police Clearance and Child Abuse Clearance: This paragraph describes the results of the search the social worker did for a police record and a child abuse record.

Recommendation and Summary: This is a short summary of the homestudy that usually includes a recommendation of whether you are fit to be an adoptive parent. Of course, it must say that you *are* able to be an adoptive parent or you cannot proceed.

A notarized copy of the homestudy is sent by the social worker to the BCIS to be connected with your I-600A application. They cannot approve your I-600A application and issue your form I-171 (your pre-approval from the BCIS) without the homestudy.

DOSSIER

The homestudy also becomes part of your "dossier," which is a group of documents required by the country from which you are adopting. Many of the same documents required for your homestudy must be included in the dossier. Most often, the dossier is translated into the proper language. The cost of the translation of the dossier is usually included in the "in-country" fee. For most international adoptions, the agency will ask you for all of the papers necessary for the dossier, and once compiled and thoroughly reviewed, they will be sent to the in-country adoption facilitator.

At the time of my adoptions, most of the documents for a Vietnamese dossier had to be "gold-seal" notarized, which means that the notary's seal must be imprinted on a gold-seal sticker that appears on the documents. I carried in my briefcase a box of gold seals as I went through the process. This may seem like a silly rule, but it's just an example of the way some countries require things to be done. I have also heard of instances in which the notary's commission expired after the papers were signed but before the adoption took place and the in-country personnel rejected those documents. It is best to choose a notary whose commission extends well into the future.

Obviously, the paperwork you need to travel to pick up your child can be overwhelming, but manageable. I got mine ready in about two months. You can go as fast or as slow as you want when preparing all that is needed. I was forty-two when I went through this process and time was a factor. For some, preparing the paperwork slowly may be helpful to provide more time to clarify their decision or prepare their homes. It is best to do your paperwork at your own pace.

After your dossier and the BCIS form I-171 are submitted to the in-country facilitator and translations are completed, you wait for a referral. In Vietnam, these can come quickly, currently one month or less, depending on the agency you choose. In other countries, the wait can be up to one year or sometimes even longer. In China, for instance, the orphanage must make some attempts to find the birth mother for up to one year. After that, the child is available for adoption. Many children coming out of China are thus usually age one year or older. A referral may be made to an adopting parent before the child is one, but he or she is usually only adoptable after the first birthday.

MEDICAL REPORTS

Along with your referral should come a medical report and a photo of the child and an approximate travel date. The photo is possibly the most powerful item that passes between the parties in the adoption process. When you first see a photo (now, it is usually on a computer screen), you find yourself saying, "Oh my God, isn't she or he beautiful?" In my case, Don sent me three photos with some paperwork by overnight mail and I looked at them over and over again. I showed them to family and friends and guarded them with great care. In one of the photos, Andy was wearing dainty mittens. Already, I discovered that I was a worrying parent, because I sent a message to Don, asking if the baby had all of his fingers and toes—not that it would have mattered if he didn't. I got a quick response saying that he did, and that the mittens are put on newborns to protect them from scratching themselves. I realized then that, through telecommunication from afar, I was doing my own version of counting fingers and toes that biological parents do while marveling over their newborn child.

The medical reports are often cryptic. They may include words such as "healthy boy" or "no physical problems." They may have the results of several blood tests, such as for hepatitis, syphilis, and HIV. This is where your leap of faith begins. How can you trust these simple words and/or results on a piece of paper that is supposed to describe the relative health of your child of whom you may have only one picture? For me, I had to trust the document and realize that it is better than no medical report at all. I know that I could not fully trust these results until I got back to the United States and had Andy and Vincent tested by their pediatrician. I also knew that most of the babies coming out of Vietnam are healthy, so that was in my favor.

Some parents may ask for another referral after reviewing a medical report, because for whatever reason, they could not take that child. If an infant, once in the system, he or she most likely will be adopted by someone. Adopting is extremely personal and if it doesn't feel right, the adopting parent(s) should wait until it does. The downside is that you'll have to wait a bit longer and/or your agency may become a little impatient with you if this happens a few times. Your homestudy should be the overriding document, however, because you were clear about what you wanted and what you could handle. During the homestudy process is when these decisions should be made, not later. If you feel pressured by your agency to take an unhealthy child, refer back to your homestudy to look at how you felt at the beginning of the process.

Hopefully you will get an approximate travel date with your referral. This will allow you to plan your trip; notify your employer, friends, and relatives; and finalize day care upon return, if needed. You should expect delays. Most of the countries sending children to the United States are developing countries, and you cannot expect their bureaucracies to work as they would in the United States. If your travel date is delayed here, rather than over there, consider yourself lucky because hotel costs will quickly add up and so will your time away from work. The in-country staff working on your adoption knows when to give you the green light to travel.

Once I arrived in Vietnam on my second trip, I was reunited with Andy within hours. Then, however, I found out that a crucial piece of my paperwork was not yet ready. Don sounded serious when he told me about it, stating that someone working in the office who prepares this document died a week before and the whole department was in mourning for two weeks. No adoption papers were being issued. Adoption is considered a happy event and there can be no happy events during the mourning period. This made me anxious, but I am an optimist and kept encouraging Don to push, so we did. One week later, we had our Giving and Receiving ceremony during which Andy became my son. This kind of delay may sound unusual but is typical of the kinds of things that can happen. I could have stayed home for five more days, but, in the end, five days was not a significant delay. Luckily, I was with Andy the entire time.

BCIS (FORMERLY THE INS)

When I adopted Andy, there was no U.S. immigration processing in Vietnam. Usually this is done at the U.S. embassy in the capital of the country. In Vietnam, the capital is Hanoi and that is where the U.S. embassy is, but they do not process adoption visas there either. Now a fully operational U.S. visa section is housed at the U.S. consulate in Ho Chi Minh City so new parents no longer have to go to Bangkok, as we did. We spent five days in Bangkok where we were told to go to the British hospital to have Andy checked by a doctor. Once we got certification that his health was OK, we were able to have our appointment with the INS at the U.S. embassy. About a dozen other parents were there to adopt Vietnamese babies, but, and perhaps I was biased, Andy was the cutest one there.

The following day, we went to the Orderly Departure Program (ODP) office to pick up a large packet of paperwork to be presented to an INS official in Chicago, our first port of entry in the United States. This packet of paperwork, which I was told not to open, started the ball rolling for Andy's permanent resident alien (green) card. He had a stamp in his Vietnamese passport, which allowed him to stay in the United States for one year from the date of arrival. During that year, he received his green card in the mail. He could maintain this status for as long as he or I chose, but I decided to have him become a U.S. citizen as soon as possible. I filed the naturalization form for adopted children, and about six months later, I received an "interview" date in the mail. I did not know that he would become a U.S. citizen that day; I presumed there would be more to it. All was in order, however, and he became a U.S. citizen shortly after his second birthday. Since February 27, 2001, the process of naturalizing children adopted abroad is no longer necessary, as they become U.S. citizens when they reach U.S. soil (and pass through Immigration). A certification of citizenship, the only real proof of citizenship, is still available from the BCIS if a parent would like to have one, but it is not necessary (unless you plan to move overseas). The cost is currently $145. A U.S. passport is about $70 and, for most needs, fulfills the same purpose. When you pick up your visa at the embassy in the country you are adopting from, they usually will give you a passport application.

Thus ends the paperwork, except for preschool applications and the occasional medical form. Andy and Vincent are my sons and U.S. citizens and no one can change that. If I had to, I would have prepared double or triple the paperwork to adopt them.

Chapter 6

How I Chose Vietnam—
Destiny's Children

After I got home from Vietnam with Andy we took a lot of walks. It was the beginning of fall, which is my favorite time of year. I ran into Jeff, a friend of a friend, who seemed very interested in my adoption. He said he'd like to talk to me about it sometime. I suggested that he and Andy and I have dinner some evening. We did and I gave him phone numbers, a newsletter, and a few Web sites about adoption. More than a year later, another mutual friend asked if I'd seen Jeff and his son lately. I responded, "His son?" Jeff had adopted a thirteen-year-old boy from North Carolina who had been in foster care for the past six years. I was surprised and thrilled. I called Jeff and he told me that the dinner we had shared over a year before had started him down a path that joined him and Joey as father and son. He said that he had told Joey about me and that he'd like to introduce us sometime soon.

I believe you call it fate or destiny that Andy, Vincent, and I or Joey and Jeff are joined as fathers and sons. Whatever the powers of the universe in motion that cause these great connections are the most fascinating part of this process. Pregnancy, in and of itself, is powerful, but when you ask why, the answer is clear. When you've been connected to an infant across the world or a teenager in the next state, you ask why, and the answer is anything but clear.

Everyone's adoption experience is different. It seems that everyone begins by thinking about making a decision to adopt. You then start doing your homework and researching all of your options. Your research may include adoption agency workshops, books, research on the Internet, such as subscribing to listservs, and so on. I know a gay couple who adopted twins by placing an ad in *Rolling Stone* magazine for over a year until they connected with a birth mother. Some of the most worthwhile research is simply talking to friends and other dads who have adopted.

Some choose to go the domestic route and some choose to go overseas, and each has advantages and disadvantages. Domestic adoptions are sometimes cheaper, especially if it is a "public adoption," which means adopting through your city or state government. These can cost as little as $5,000 and sometimes are free if the child is disabled or ill. Some domestic adoptions can be "independent" adoptions, which do not involve an agency or a government. An adoption attorney might be needed for an independent adoption. The most difficult part of domestic adoptions is finding a birth mother.

Some of today's domestic adoptions are called "open adoptions," where the birth mother and possibly the biological father want to remain in contact with the child and his or her new parents. Some adopting parents are fine with this arrangement, but others feel it may be complicated and confusing for the child.

Others with whom I have spoken want to adopt domestically because they feel that plenty of children right here in the United States need homes—why go overseas? Others just don't want to travel overseas and/or file the extra paperwork required by the BCIS.

As water seeks its own level, adopting parents who do their research will find the path to becoming parents that best fits them.

I chose early to focus on an international adoption. I filed the INS request for a form I-171 as soon as I started my homestudy. The main reason I chose to go overseas for a child was time. From what I read, an international adoption meant I could be a father within a year, while domestic adoptions seemed to take longer.

WHAT COUNTRIES ALLOW SINGLE MEN TO ADOPT?

I started researching which countries would allow single men to adopt—at the time of my adoption I was aware of only five. Almost all countries with active adoption programs will allow single women to adopt, but only a handful allow single men. Guatemala, China, Russia, Vietnam, and Cambodia were my options. (The Ukraine is now an option for single men.) In some ways, my task was easier having only those five choices, and I was able to research all of these countries at the same time. Though my first interest was Russia, I did some investigation and spoke with a few friends and agencies. I kept hearing that health was an issue for Russian babies, due to a high incidence of fetal alcohol syndrome, and as a single parent, I needed to focus on a healthy infant.

I then looked at China. Although most of the children coming out of China are girls, some boys are available and are usually given to single males. However, at the time I was adopting, the Chinese required all single adopting parents, male and female, to sign an affidavit saying they were not gay or lesbian. I felt that if I could avoid lying, I should. Unfortunately, this rule is still in effect for individuals adopting in China.

Since I adopted Andy, I've learned more about why so many girls are available in China. At weddings, a common congratulatory remark is "Happy marriage and have a healthy boy." In the rural areas of China, a family is allowed to have two children only if the first one is a girl. This is a government-sanctioned policy that perpetuates the notion that boys are better. Some families feel they need a boy for help around the farm or the family business, whatever that may be. Women in these families often hide their pregnancies until birth and abandon the baby girls. I met a single mom of a Chinese girl at a flea market a while back, and she asked whether I knew Andy's birth date. I do; I have the birth certificate. She knows her daughter's birth date only because it was pinned to the baby's blanket when she was abandoned in the woods. Apparently, throughout rural China, babies are left in certain locations for social workers to pick up and take to an orphanage. Usually a search is conducted for the birth mother in an attempt to reunite her with her baby, but if that fails, the baby is available for adoption after one year. This is the reason that many children from China are over one year old before they are adopted.

I was signed on to the listserv for Guatemala adoptions. I did not see any messages from single men who had adopted, so I put a message on the list asking if single-male adoptions were possible in Guatemala and, if so, what agencies should be contacted. A long response from one person indicated that single men could adopt from Guatemala as long as they were not homosexual. I decided that I didn't want to hide who I was and/or be under suspicion. I have since met two male couples who adopted their sons from Guatemala and did not speak of any real difficulties, other than the normal ones we all experience. Guatemala can be a great choice for some because it is so close to the United States and you generally are required to go only once.

As I researched all of these countries simultaneously, I was able to eliminate those with which I was uncomfortable. Vietnam and Cambodia didn't have any apparent restrictions about gay people adopting, and the timing of the adoption process in each was pretty fast, from what I'd heard. My homestudy was done, and I was a week away from receiving my INS preapproval for adopting a foreign child. When looking for agencies that had programs in Vietnam and Cambodia, I saw the message from Don (whom I did not know at the time) on the Vietnam listserv. I responded to him, which was the start of my adoption of Andrew, and I stopped my research. That is how I ended up in Vietnam to adopt Andy, and later Vincent. I really believe that destiny had a great deal to do with our being paired as father and sons. I now think of Vietnam as my second country of origin, much more so than Ireland. Somehow it has crept into my being because I am a father of two of its sons.

I did my adoption follow-up work with the same agency that did my homestudy. Linda, the social worker, commented that Andy and I have the same disposition. I took this as a compliment because Andy is very good-natured and calm (and so is Vincent). Perhaps destiny is more than just connecting people as family. Whoever matched me with my sons did so with care.

Chapter 7

The Bottom Line—
How Much Will It Cost?

Very few of my co-workers have young kids, so I was happy to hear of my closest colleague's pregnancy. After she had the baby, she expressed an interest in adoption for her second child because, as she said, so many children need homes. I explained to her some of the costs. I paid about $20,000 for my adoption of Andy and got an adoption tax credit of about $4,000, so the net cost was $16,000. She paid one $10 copay during her first doctor's office visit and never paid another dime. She has a beautiful little boy too.

The money seems absolutely secondary when adopting. Each time I adopted, I hoped that I had enough and made a mental plan of how I would make each payment when it was due. The goal of being a father, however, was strangely disconnected from the outflow of funds from my checking account. I knew ahead of time approximately what it would cost and my expenses did not go over that amount. If they had, I might have a different take on the money issue, but, as it turned out, the money was basically just like the paperwork—obtain this document or pay this fee and one day be united with a child to raise. I heard of many stories about expenses escalating beyond the adopting parents' control, and I heard of money paid for nothing, but most of the people around me who adopted incurred a steady course of expected payments.

Generally, a foreign adoption can cost anywhere from $15,000 to $30,000, and that includes your travel expenses. The fees go to various places that I will detail in this chapter. A domestic adoption can be much less expensive, especially if you go the public route. In some states, if you choose a special-needs child, the expenses are sometimes waived. In some cases, you can even get a sustenance payment for raising a child with special needs.

The federal tax credit for adoption increased in January 2002. Any adoption (international or domestic) that becomes final after January 1, 2002, is eligible for a tax credit of up to $10,000. If your income is higher than $150,000, the credit becomes gradually smaller. This means that if you spend $21,000 on your adoption, the net cost to you after a few years would be $11,000. I stipulate after a few years because you don't get a giant refund in the year you adopt; you have to carry the remaining credit forward for a few years to offset your tax liability, but the net effect would be $10,000 back in your pocket. (It is not a tax deduction, but a credit, which is much better than a deduction.)

The following are the costs I incurred for the adoption of Andy by month:

> March—Fee to INS for processing the I-600A: $125 (has since increased to $460); homestudy fee: $1,200
>
> May—Agency fee: $1,650 (reduced from the normal fee of $3,000 because I had already located a child—includes application fee of $150)
>
> June—Travel costs for first trip: hotel $300, airfare $1,700; first installment of in-country fee: $2,500; second installment of in-country fee: $2,400
>
> August—Remaining in-country fee: $4,900; travel expenses: hotel $1,700, airfare $2,280 (included Andy's flight home); INS visa fee: $350
>
> September—Follow-up report (adoption agency fee): $550; re-adoption fee for District of Columbia: $80
>
> November—INS naturalization fee: $125
>
> *Total:* $19,860

If you are going overseas for a child, your first expense will be the BCIS fee to process your I-600A, the advance processing application required to gain approval to bring a foreign-born child into the United States. The fee is currently $460 plus a fingerprint charge of $50 per adult household member. You pay these two fees at the same time and then you get an appointment for fingerprinting. The BCIS will not approve your I-600A until they have a notarized copy of your homestudy, which is usually done concurrently with the I-600A processing.

The homestudy fee is usually paid before the homestudy starts and ranges from about $800 to $1,500, depending on the agency and where you live. This fee covers the social worker's time for gathering all of the documents needed, visiting your home, and meeting with you two other times. You may also need to pay a fee for a police clearance or child abuse clearance, depending on your state.

The agency fee is the amount you pay an agency for processing your adoption paperwork and to be an advocate for you when you hit any snags (and you will). The agency I used for Andy's adoption charged $3,000 at the time. They gave me a 50 percent discount because I had already been connected to the adoption facilitator in Vietnam. I could have just done an "independent adoption" through him, but I wanted some assurance that if this adoption did not go through, the in-country fee that I had already paid would not be lost. They gave me that assurance in writing, so basically I spent $1,500 as insurance on the rest of the funds and for some assistance with the paperwork. The agency I worked with for my second adoption charged a $4,000 agency fee. The fees are worthwhile, especially if something goes wrong. A credible adoption agency will advocate for you and try within their powers to resolve issues that arise. Sometimes these issues are small and can be handled within a day, but sometimes they require more time or legal intervention. These are often the emotional issues. You are in a very vulnerable position once you've come this far and you've seen a picture of your child or met him or her.

Adoption agencies can be nonprofit or for-profit corporations. A nonprofit agency will have a board of directors that oversees the executive director. Usually, in for-profit agencies, the executive director is a principal who shares in the profits generated by the firm's business. Most nonprofit agencies' financial statements are a matter of public record, but those of for-profits are not. Getting the financial statements may not be necessary, but knowing that the agency head has to answer to someone may be reassuring. In short, when interviewing agencies, ask whether they are nonprofit or for-profit. Nonprofit agencies are business oriented, too, but accountability is generally greater with a volunteer board of directors and accessible financial statements.

Travel costs are probably the expense that will vary the most from family to family. You can go low budget or high end; the differences, of course, are flying business class versus coach or choosing a five-star over a two-star hotel. In my case, the five-star hotel cost only $80 per night. I could have stayed in Vietnam for less, say, $35 per night, but the $80-per-night hotel was my oasis. I needed that comfort on a daily basis. The business of adoption is emotionally taxing, so you'll find that creature comforts are your lifesavers. Also, adjusting to a new baby and trying to satisfy his or her needs is easier when you are in a Western-style hotel. For my second adoption, I stayed at the hotel the adoption facilitator recommended. It was $50 per night and was very comfortable. All of her adopting parents were staying there, which made things easier as well.

The in-country fee is the biggest expense in the whole process. For Vietnam, the in-country fee was $9,800 when I adopted Andy and $11,000 when I adopted Vincent. Each time I adopted, I paid the in-country fee in three installments, the third of which was due right before the second trip. I never asked my adoption facilitators where the money went, but I could see that the people working on my case were busy all the time. I left Vietnam each time thinking that I got good value for my in-country fee after meeting all of the people involved in the process. I never saw any bribes being handed over, except the occasional carton of cigarettes or box of "mooncakes." Theoretically, an in-country fee should never be paid twice. That is, if for some reason the adoption does not go through as planned, the agency or adoption facilitator should offer another referral without asking for another in-country fee.

Chapter 8

The Current Laws on Gay Parenting in Each State

When I first walked into the agency that did my homestudy for Andy I told them outright that I am a single gay man. That meeting took place in Alexandria, Virginia, a mere five miles from my home in Washington, DC. The social worker and the woman who ran the agency said that being gay had no relevance to my adoption and therefore would not be a part of my homestudy. They welcomed and encouraged me. I left there more confident about my dreams, not so worried about the gay issue, and wondering from what country to adopt. At the time, the laws in Washington, DC, were very liberal for gay parenting (and still are). Partners could adopt their partners' children through second-parent adoption. Adopting as a single guy was legal and easy. In Virginia, where the meeting took place, adopting as a gay parent was not so easy. Although it was not illegal for gay people to adopt, the climate was not as favorable in Virginia as it was in DC, especially if two adults of the same sex were living in the home. Crossing the river back to DC that day, I realized that, symbolically (at least in the context of adoptions for gay people), I was crossing the bridge between the North and the South. I have since moved to Virginia (better schools, bigger yard), so I am living in a state with a conservative climate for gay adoptions. So far, it has not affected me. If I have a partner someday, I would probably move back to Washington, DC, just to have him become a legal parent.

State laws for adopting as a gay parent vary greatly. A handful of states have passed laws making it illegal for gay people to adopt. Thankfully, more than three times as many states permit adoptions by gay people and some of those allow second-parent adoption. All of the state-by-state information in this chapter was derived from the Human Rights Campaign's (HRC) FamilyNet Web site (www.hrc.

org/familynet). It is reprinted here by permission of the Human
Rights Campaign Foundation. FamilyNet is a great resource for adoption information and for gay-parenting issues in general. It provides
legal forms and information for partners and parents for recording
their intentions concerning finances, health, property, and custody, as
well as a region-by-region list of gay-friendly adoption agencies. The
site also includes articles on current events involving gay-parenting
issues. The information on adoption and parenting changes constantly across the country, so I encourage adopting parents to check
the FamilyNet Web site for the current status in their states. Although
some case law is listed for some states, it often involves custody issues for biological children when at least one of the parents is gay.
Not many adoptions by gay parents have been tested in courts, perhaps because many parents choose just to be parents and not make a
statement.

A note for those adopting internationally: When you've adopted
overseas, the adoption is considered final in the eyes of the two countries and the international community. When you return to the United
States and submit your child's visa upon entry, your child automati-
cally becomes a U.S. citizen. A follow-up adoption in the state or ju-
risdiction in which you live is recommended sometime before your
child enters school, but it is not necessary in all states. If you are planning to move to a state that has more favorable adoption laws for gay
parents (such as allowing second-parent adoptions), you may choose
to wait until you have moved to finalize the adoption of your
child(ren), unless certain state statutes require otherwise. Conversely,
of course, if you live in a state that allows gay couples to adopt and/or
second-parent adoptions, you would want to act quickly to finalize
the adoption. Sometimes state laws change, and though usually for
the better for gay people, it can go in the other direction.

The following is a brief summary of the laws for gay and lesbian
adopting and parenting for the fifty states and the District of Columbia.

Completely Legal

Lesbian and gay couples and individuals are permitted to adopt in
California, Connecticut, Illinois, Massachusetts, New Jersey, New
York, Pennsylvania, Vermont, and Washington, DC. Second-parent
adoption is also legal statewide for all of these states, except in Cali-

fornia and New Jersey, where it is determined county by county, or case by case. In California, state law now gives registered partners the right for one partner to adopt the other partner's child as a stepparent. In 1997, New Jersey became the first state to allow same-sex partners to jointly adopt children in state care.

Favorable Climate

The climate is generally favorable for lesbian and gay couples and individuals to adopt in Colorado, Delaware, Maryland, Michigan, Oregon, Rhode Island, and Washington, and in some counties, second-parent adoption has also been granted. However, an attempt is currently under way to stop all second-parent adoptions in Michigan.

Gay individuals (single parents) can adopt in Ohio, but second-parent adoption is not allowed.

Illegal

Laws forbidding adoption by gay individuals or couples exist in Florida, Mississippi, and Utah. Adoption by gay couples is also forbidden by law in Kentucky, but gay individuals might be able to adopt (case by case). It also appears, from a review of case law, that it is illegal in Wisconsin for gay couples to adopt, and the climate is similarly unfavorable for gay individuals, although there is anecdotal evidence that gay individuals have adopted in Wisconsin.

Mixed Success

- Alaska: Gay individuals have adopted and some second-parent adoptions have been granted in several counties in Alaska.
- Indiana: There is anecdotal evidence of gay individuals adopting in Indiana. Second-parent adoptions by some courts have been granted in Indiana with mixed rulings for custody disputes involving one parent who is gay.
- Iowa: Reportedly, second-parent adoptions have been granted in Iowa, with mixed rulings for custody disputes involving one parent who is gay.
- Minnesota: Although the climate for gay parenting is still unclear statewide, gay individuals can adopt, and some counties in Minnesota have approved second-parent adoptions.

- Nevada: Second-parent adoptions have been granted in some lower courts in Nevada, but no specific case law or statutes support gay or lesbian adoptions.
- New Mexico: Second-parent adoptions have been granted in New Mexico, with a number of favorable rulings in custody disputes involving one parent who is gay.
- North Carolina: There is anecdotal evidence of gay individuals adopting in North Carolina but no case law for gay and lesbian adoptions. Records show some unfavorable decisions in custody cases involving one parent who is gay.
- Tennessee: Gay individuals are often able to adopt in Tennessee, but it is unclear whether second-parent adoptions would be granted.
- Texas: The state adoption policy in Texas discourages discrimination against gay people, but judges tend to do it anyway, as shown by court records. Some judges, however, have approved adoptions for gay individuals and couples as well as second-parent adoptions.

No Reported Cases, but Possible Favorable Climate

- Alabama: Reportedly, lesbian and gay individuals have adopted in Alabama, but the prospect for gay couples is not as favorable based on custody cases.
- Hawaii: There are no reported cases of gay people adopting in Hawaii, but a family court judge approved second-parent adoptions for three lesbian couples in 2000. One of the mothers in each couple was the biological mother, so what effect this will have on joint adoptions in which neither partner is a biological parent is still unknown.
- Maine: Some favorable rulings in custody cases involving gay parents in Maine indicate a favorable climate, but there are no specific cases for adoptions by gay parents.
- Missouri: There are no reported cases of adoptions by gay parents, but a recent favorable ruling by the Missouri Court of Appeals in a custody dispute indicates a shift in acceptance of gay parenting.
- New Hampshire: In 1999, the governor of New Hampshire overturned a prohibition on adoption and foster parenting by

gay people. Second-parent adoptions have been granted in some counties.

- South Carolina: Although having no reported cases of adoptions by gay parents, South Carolina has had some favorable rulings for custody and visitation disputes involving one parent who is gay.
- West Virginia: Adoptions are not part of the public record in West Virginia, so it is unclear whether gay people are able to adopt. A recent custody dispute ruling, however, was favorable for a lesbian mother.

No Reported Cases, Unknown Climate

In addition to no reported cases of gay men or lesbians adopting in Kansas, Idaho, Georgia, Montana, South Dakota, and Wyoming, it is unclear whether judges in these states would discriminate based on sexual orientation.

No Reported Cases, Possible Unfavorable Climate

Again, there are no reported cases of gay men or lesbians adopting in Arizona, Arkansas, North Dakota, and Virginia, and it is unclear whether judges in these states would discriminate based on sexual orientation. However, the case law for custody and visitation disputes when one parent is gay has been less than favorable for the gay parent.

There is anecdotal evidence of lesbian and gay people adopting in individual and second-parent contexts in Arizona. In North Dakota, there is some anecdotal evidence of second-parent adoptions. Historically, Virginia has had an unfavorable climate for gay parents, but a recent settlement may allow greater positive possibilities for gay parents.

No Reported Cases, Special Restrictions

Similarly, along with no reported cases of gay men or lesbians adopting in Louisiana, Nebraska, and Oklahoma, it is unclear whether judges in these states would discriminate based on sexual orientation. Because the state adoption statute in Louisiana restricts adoption to married couples and single individuals, it is unlikely that a gay couple could adopt jointly. In Nebraska, the Department of Social

Services bans lesbian and gay people from becoming foster parents. In Oklahoma, in 1999, a bill passed that would bar gay and lesbian people from adopting through the state's Child Protective Services agency.

If Second-Parent Adoption Is Not Available in Your State

If second-parent adoption is unavailable where you live, you should prepare a written coparenting agreement or a custody agreement with your partner. (Coparenting agreements state that while only one of you is considered the legal parent, both of you consider yourselves equal coparents with shared rights and responsibilities to care for your child. Such agreements also specify how the couple will share custody in the event of a breakup and how they would manage disputes.) At least, you should gather other evidence that proves you are a family. It is important to recognize that these steps are not guaranteed to secure your parental rights because courts are not required to uphold such agreements. Still, many attorneys recommend that you complete such agreements anyway to demonstrate your intention to the court in the event a custody dispute develops. Because family law varies from state to state, it is recommended that you consult an attorney familiar with these issues in your state for help drawing up such documents. If you are unable to do so, however, you still can compose one on your own that may withstand a legal dispute as long as you and your partner both sign and date it and preferably have it witnessed and/or notarized.

Again, I recommend checking the FamilyNet Web site for recent updates, or check with one of the adoption agencies recommended by HRC. If none are listed for your state, call one of the agencies nearest to you—they may have some answers for your situation. As with any endeavor as important as adoption, an attorney may be able to help you navigate the legal bureaucracy, or if confronted by antigay sentiments along the way.

Chapter 9

Other Ways of Becoming a Gay Dad

My friend Richard has two children from a previous marriage. Whenever we get together with other gay dads, he is sometimes asked whether his children are biologically his or adopted. He explains that he got them the traditional way, which, he quickly jokes, is nontraditional in this group.

Most of my gay male friends with kids have adopted them. It clearly is the most popular way for gay men to become dads, but it is not the only way. I've seen many gay men struggle with the question of how they will become fathers. Again, this decision is personal; no one can tell you which course to choose.

Of course, you can have kids the traditional way, as did Richard, but then you might have to share them with your ex-wife. Surrogacy, which allows you to carry on your genetic heritage, is another option. You could also consider coparenting with a single woman or lesbian couple.

SURROGACY

Most gay men considering parenthood think the biggest advantage of surrogacy is the biological connection. For some, carrying on their genes is very important. Some gay men feel family pressure, perceived or real, that a biological child would be more accepted by the extended family. Also, many gay men may worry that their parents and/or siblings may not accept a child of their gay son or brother because the thought of them being a father is shocking—like coming out all over again: "Let's sit down at the kitchen table again, as we did twenty years ago; I have something to tell you." Your relatives might think that men don't raise babies, women do. Also, they may wonder what it will be like for their grandchild to be raised by a gay parent or two gay parents. Then, imagine telling them that the child may be from another country and/or another race. You are delivering a lot of news for them to digest. Perhaps having a child through a surrogate mother will soften the blow or at least make the issues less intense. It is best to make *your* decision to suit *your* needs. If you choose to have a child through surrogacy, it should be because *you* need to have your own biological child.

I never seriously considered surrogacy. I've never had the desire to have a biological child. Again, I emphasize that this decision is extremely personal. I chose to adopt my children because many kids out there need homes, and if I can provide a home to a child, then I will. This may seem philanthropic, I admit, but if I can do that along with satisfying my parental instincts, then why not? The notion of saving a child is a noble one, but it should not be the primary reason for adopting. After having Andy for a few years, I can say without reservation that the lack of a biological connection to me has nothing to do with the amount of love I have for him.

The cost of surrogacy can vary widely. The least expensive route to take would be to find a surrogate mother on your own who is willing to go through the process for a fee, which will compensate her for lost work and other expenses during her pregnancy. Medical costs for artificial inseminations can range from almost nothing to somewhat costly if you have it done in a clinic. If you choose this route, the birth mother may have the right to keep the baby after he or she is born (depending on the laws in your state), despite the terms of the contract you have signed with her. Alternatively, you can buy eggs from an anonymous donor, fertilize them outside the womb with your semen, and then have them implanted in a birth mother. This is called in vitro fertilization (creating a test-tube baby). This method carries less risk that the birth mother will be able to claim rights to the baby, but it is much more expensive; for each time the eggs are fertilized and implanted, the fee can range from $2,000 to $4,000.

You can hire a surrogacy firm to do all of the legwork for you. They can search for a birth mother and may have several waiting birth mothers who will carry your child. In Los Angeles, one surrogacy firm (Growing Generations) caters solely to the gay community. These arrangements, however, can be very expensive, ranging from $40,000 to $80,000, depending on whether you artificially inseminate a birth mother using her eggs, or buy eggs from a donor and have them implanted. Obviously, the more false starts you have, the more it will cost you.

Another factor to consider is time. When you are adopting, depending on the country you choose, you can have a child within a year. Surrogacy may take more time, easily over one year.

COPARENTING

The traditional definition of coparenting is that a man and a woman who have a platonic relationship get together and decide to have and raise a baby. Usually, they are not married and do not live together, so the child may have two homes, depending on the arrangement. Obviously the different levels of commitment (emotional, financial, and practical) on the parts of the biological parents are usually spelled out in advance. Sometimes a contract is drawn up, and sometimes not. Sometimes the biological father is comfortable with a "close uncle" role, and sometimes he is involved at a 50 percent level in the duties of raising the child. Conversely, the father can be the primary caregiver and the biological mother a "close aunt." Some coparenting situations turn out to be different from what was originally agreed upon before the baby was born, and some become difficult because of geography or strained relationships between the parents. I have met gay guys who never really considered parenthood until they were approached by a woman who wanted a sperm donation. These men usually are happy with the close uncle role.

Provided the mother has health insurance, the costs of having a child in a coparenting arrangement can be minimal, as artificial inseminations can be done at home. Raising the child, however, has costs, and this arrangement should be spelled out before the baby is born. Some mothers who are the primary caregivers in a coparenting situation want no financial help from the fathers. This would indicate support in the event of a custody battle. Conversely, one of the parents may ask for financial support without allowing custody or visitation rights. If the mother is the primary caregiver, the biological father may be saddled with child support without having custody rights. The opposite can also be true, but not very common. Unless you choose to have the father listed as "unknown" on the birth certificate, both biological parents will be considered parents of the child per most state laws. Of course, custody rights and support payments are defined by your state's law, which may or may not have been tested by a co-parenting arrangement.

Coparenting can be a great way to carry on one's genetic heritage. Also, it can be a wonderful way to share the duties of parenthood without sacrificing all of your freedom. Regardless of the situation and the intentions of the people involved, the decision is a serious one. Relationships and people change, so it is important to remain flexible and adapt to the ever-changing needs of the child and the other coparent. When compared to adoption or surrogacy, coparent-ing has a completely different set of issues and complications, but the end result, hopefully, will be the same rewards—the joy of being a parent and having an influence on a child's life.

Chapter 10

Big Decisions

The biggest decision, of course, is whether to become a parent. Once that decision has been made, other important decisions follow. Many of these are personal decisions that can be made by only you (and your partner, if you have one).

BOY OR GIRL?

Obviously, this decision is deeply personal. I can impart only my experience as I chose to adopt boys. When you are adopting, you can choose the sex in most cases. Some parents choose to say "first available," which is basically the same attitude of biological expectant parents—they will be happy no matter what. Both of my homestudies were written for adopting a boy. A homestudy does not have to mention a sex preference, but if you have one you should include that information. In the world of adoptions, girls are more in demand than boys. Aside from China (most of the time), the wait is longer if you prefer a girl.

My choice of a boy centered around my belief that I would simply be better at raising a boy throughout the years. I have much more confidence in my ability to nurture him for sports and typical boys' activities than I would have with a girl. I've always wanted a son, so it was natural for me to request a boy. When my homestudy was complete, my sister asked me why I didn't want a girl. She said that the bond between a little girl and her daddy was like no other. I could have had either of my homestudies changed to request a girl, but I was convinced that a boy was best for me. I did, however, consider that having a gay dad might be easier on a teenage girl than a teenage boy. A girl might think it is cool to have a gay dad or two gay dads, while a boy might find it tougher to get through those hurdles. In the end, though, I went with my gut instinct and each time requested a boy.

BABY, TODDLER, OR OLDER CHILD?

Again, this is strictly a personal decision, but I can impart my feelings on why I chose to adopt two infants. My reasons center on the concept of "attachment." I was under the impression that the younger the child, the easier it is for him or her to attach to me. Nonattachment, I felt, would mean trouble, especially down the road. I wanted my children to feel a strong sense of belonging to our family. I did some research on the attachment issue and discovered that generally, children under two years old have no trouble attaching to their adoptive parents. I decided to use that as my absolute upper limit, but I requested under one year old, if available. In my mind, I welcomed all the chores and joys that accompany parenting an infant. I adopted Andy when he was four and a half months old and Vincent when he was seven months old. They've attached to me in mighty powerful and emotional ways.

TRANSRACIAL ADOPTION?

Having a child who is of a different race can be a sensitive issue, but, so far, this has been a nonissue in our family. No one has ever said anything negative about our being different, and I hope no one ever will. As a matter of fact, people are so cautious that they usually don't even ask my children's nationality. I think they feel that I might be offended if they recognize our differences. We do get some looks wherever we go, but as fast as people do a double take, they look away and go about their business. I have thought about the eventuality of being asked questions about my children's origins when they are able to hear and understand them. I hope I will always remember to consider their feelings first when talking about our differences. Even if someone asks an insensitive question, I will refrain from making a scene to protect Andy and Vincent from any hurt feelings. Their feelings come first in these situations. On the other hand, Andy now says he is from Vietnam with some excitement, so I will continue to encourage this as a source of pride for him and Vincent.

That Andy and Vincent are from a different race makes absolutely no difference to me, and I realized this when I first saw a photo of Andy. I have been connected to these children because they need a home and I have a home for them—it is as simple as that. Destiny brought us together. Whatever bigotry is out there is in other people's hearts and minds, not in ours. I hope that I will be able to pass these principles on to my sons, so they will be able to let any prejudices (concerning the race or the gay issue) roll off their backs. I don't pretend to think that we will not have problems as they grow up, but I consider race a small enough issue that we will come through any trials with more strength and resolve.

If you adopt a child of a different race, your community may be a factor in how you are treated. As gay people, we know that large cities are generally more socially liberal. The same comforts we look for in our communities as gay people hopefully also will support transracial adoption.

DOMESTIC OR INTERNATIONAL?

When I started my adoption process, I briefly checked the adoption programs available in my community. Many children in foster care are in need of homes. In some cases, the birth parents want to be a part of the child's life; that is an open adoption. Babies are less plentiful than older children with domestic adoptions. At the same time, I was doing research on the handful of countries that allow single men to adopt. I knew in my heart that I wanted to go overseas for a child but thought I'd better at least check the local situation. Part of the reason I was convinced that the overseas option was best for me was the birth mother's lack of involvement. I knew that the chances of the biological parents contacting us would be remote. I felt that it would be less confusing for my children if their biological parents were not involved in their lives. Certainly, I consider this a personal decision as well.

HOW OLD IS TOO OLD?

At the time of my adoption, my age was a significant issue for me. I was forty-two when I first became serious about adopting. I thought I would adopt a three-year-old, so that I would be younger than sixty when he went to college. I was focusing on that rather than on the unknown of where the child has been for his first three years. I spoke to several people about this. I remember my brother's comments best. He had just become the father of twins a year earlier and he said, "If you can get a baby—get a baby." He said his kids' brains are on "turbo" right now. He convinced me that the first few years are extremely important in children's lives. He encouraged me not to miss them. As a single parent, I was concerned about mental health and the effects of a long stay in an orphanage. Suddenly, the difference of one, two, or three years did not seem so important. What is the real difference if you are sixty or sixty-two at your child's high school graduation? A friend of mine who is fifty-five and his partner (who is thirty-seven) just got home from Vietnam with their twin sons who are about to turn one year old. Every country has age restrictions or guidelines, but no universal rule dictates how old you must be (or not be) to be a good parent. I was forty-two when I first met Andrew and forty-three when I brought him home. I was forty-five when I arrived home with Vincent. As the saying goes, you are as young as you feel, and if you feel able to parent a child you probably can, no matter what your age. I will be sixty-three when Vincent graduates from high school, and I do not consider this a problem. I am more mature now and ready and willing to handle the tasks of parenting—certainly more ready than I would have been ten or twenty years ago.

Chapter 11

Preparing for Life with a Baby or Child

Shortly before I left for my second trip to Vietnam, this time to bring Andy home, I had a date. When I first met this guy, I did not tell him that I was "in a family way." I had put Andy's crib together in my living room earlier that day, so when he walked in, he saw it but didn't say anything at first. A few minutes later, he said, "You have a crib in your living room." I then told him that I was adopting a child in the next few weeks and I showed him some of the pictures I had taken of Andy on my first visit to Vietnam. Needless to say, he was shocked, and not knowing what else to say, he joked, "All I wanted was a date!"

There is no way to become completely emotionally prepared for how your life will change. What new parent can? The best way to approach emotional readiness is to have confidence in your ability to handle what unfolds, one day at a time, in rational and loving ways. For me, that defines good parenting.

You can, however, prepare yourself in many concrete ways, including readying your home, choosing day care, planning your baby shower, knowing what to take with you on your trip, picking a name, and so forth.

BABY SHOWER

Should you have a baby shower and, if so, when? Adoptions are sometimes uncertain, so I chose to have the shower after I returned home with Andy. I scheduled it about nine days after my expected return from Vietnam, but since we were delayed for six days, we arrived home only three days before the shower. I decided not to cancel it despite significant jet lag and Andy's adjustment to a new schedule. Two of my friends had planned the shower and many friends and family were scheduled to attend, so I decided to go forward with it. It turned out to be a great party and almost everyone got to meet Andy despite his nap in the middle of the afternoon. The shower is an opportunity for you to receive encouragement from the people around you.

NAMES

Choosing a name is an important and personal decision. I do not pretend to duplicate the suggestions that are published in the many baby name books out there, but I will tell you how I chose Andrew and Vincent for the names of my sons. First and foremost, I wanted traditional names. Emotionally, I believe I am giving my sons a good sense of themselves, but I do think that they will have more identity issues than most children do, for several reasons. They have a gay dad (maybe will have two dads), they have an Irish last name, and they are a different race than I am. My children's identities are based in love, and I can already see that Andy feels good about himself—he is certainly his own person. However, I think that a child's name relates to his or her self-identity, so I chose names that are traditional and common, but not too common. I didn't want them to dislike their names someday. I checked <babynames.com>, which ranks children's names according to popularity for the past several years. Andrew was number nine on the 1997 list. I hadn't realized it was that popular, but I still liked it and its other forms, Andy and Drew. I like names that have more than one form. For Vincent, much of the same reasoning applied—I always liked the name, but it had no family significance. The church we attended when I was a kid was St. Vincent's, so that may have been an influence as well. Also, I like the short versions, Vince and Vinnie.

Andrew's Vietnamese given name was Trung Van Phuong. Trung is his surname and Phuong is his given name. In Vietnam, the last name comes first, as in China. I wanted Andy to retain part of his heritage in his name, so his middle name is Phuong. I also gave Vincent a Vietnamese middle name, Luc (pronounced "look"), meaning destiny.

How does a gay couple decide which last name to give their children? Several of my friends who are couples chose various forms of names for their children. Some hyphenated the two last names, but one couple used one of their last names (which is a common first name) as the first name for their son and the other partner's last name for the child's surname. Not all couples have this luxury, but I thought it was a nice way to recognize both parents in the name of their child.

PREPARING YOUR HOME

Most of what you need to do to prepare your home centers on safety issues. If you have a stairway, you should install a gate at the top that is built into the wall. Some gates fit into doorways but are not attached. These are fine for the bottom of the stairs but are not recommended for the top of the stairs as the baby could push them through by applying pressure on one side. The gate you buy should indicate that it is suitable for stairs. At first, with an infant, you may not need these things, but babies grow fast and yours will be crawling around before you know it.

Make some space in your kitchen for baby bottles and plastic bowls and plates. A tub in a drawer works best for the baby bottles. It's a time-saver to throw them in there when they come out of the dishwasher.

Andy was five months old when I brought him home, so I chose to make his room a little boy's room instead of a baby's room, thinking he would grow into it. I also thought this would keep me from having to repaint his room in a year or so.

YOUR TRIP

What will you need on your trip? If you are going overseas, the amount of luggage you take can be significant. Northwest Airline offers special fares and one extra bag without a fee for adoptive parents (www.nwa.com/features/adopt.shtml). It is generally not advised to take a stroller or a car seat with you if you are going overseas. If your child is younger than one year old, he or she will probably fit in a Snuggli, which is the best way to carry an infant around. It is also a good way to bond with your child by being physically close to him or her. If you feel the need for a stroller, buy one of the umbrella types after you arrive in the country and perhaps leave it behind with your adoption facilitator as a donation to their program. However, the sidewalks in most developing countries are not friendly to stroller traffic, so you may find it not so useful. Car seats are not used in many countries, so if you take one, you may find that you cannot attach it because many taxis or cars do not have seat belts in the backseat. This is another case where adoption becomes a "leap of faith" because precautions we take for granted may not always be available as you move through your journey.

In Asia, you will find children's clothing in the markets for very little cost—about US $2.00 for a matching T-shirt and shorts set. I bought some outfits for the following summer, but I wish I had bought more for when the kids get a little older. You will probably end up buying a suitcase or duffel bag to carry home all of the new baby stuff you acquire. Luggage is usually cheaper overseas than in the United States, so, again, it is not advised to carry an empty bag with you. You should, however, carry one or two outfits and a couple sets of pajamas in case you get your baby right away and are unable to go to the market beforehand. The hotels that you will stay in have air-conditioning, which may or may not be the case at the orphanage or foster care home where your child has been living. So, for your child not to be shocked by the temperature, put him or her in pajamas or keep the room a bit warmer than is usual for you. Diapers, baby wipes, bottles, and formula are available in most countries that have adoption programs, so you don't have to carry these items with you. You should check on this before you travel, however. Also, you should maintain the same formula for your baby as he or she has been eating. You don't want to add that change to the list of changes that he or she is experiencing. If you want to change the formula, wait until you get home and the baby has adjusted to his or her new surroundings. Keep in mind also that many orphanage infants are not used to wearing diapers, most likely due to economics. How they get away with this is still a mystery to me. When I took Vincent to the hotel, I started him on diapers and a boil broke out within days. His skin was not used to being confined.

While you are in your child's country, you will want to visit a doctor. My first meeting with a doctor was just about an hour after meeting Andy. I didn't know what to ask him so I kept asking him if Andy was a normal baby. He probably thought I was not normal! A couple of nights later he made a house call to my hotel room just after midnight at my request. Andy was wheezing and I was not sure why. He said it was probably just his lungs reacting and adjusting to the air-conditioning in the hotel room. So, if you meet with a doctor, get his or her number and ask if you can contact him or her while you are there. They usually don't charge much for the visit. Also ask for an after-hours emergency number. Diarrhea is very common among these children and should be addressed right away. You may even want to have some soy formula in your hotel room, as this is indicated for treatment of diarrhea in infants.

As for the water—don't drink it, although your child may be able to handle it better than you. Be very careful to drink only bottled water in any foreign country. Even though some hotels will indicate that the water is potable, it is best not to rely on that information. Obtain from the hotel front desk a pot for boiling water, and use the boiled water for mixing your baby's formula.

DAY CARE

For many, this may be the single biggest reason they cannot adopt. If you are single, the financial burden is yours alone and it can be very expensive. I started my research early, while I was preparing my home-study and dossier documents. Timing is very important, as nanny availability is dependent on departure from the employ of other parents. I put an ad on a bulletin board in my neighborhood with approximate starting dates and I received a few inquiries. I hired one of the nannies who answered my ad to come to my house every day. She lived only one block away. It was easier for Andy to stay home all day and I felt it was the best situation for the first year or so.

Nannies can cost anywhere between $200 and $500 per week depending on their duties. The more household chores required such as cooking, cleaning, or laundry, the more they will charge. Day care is not quite as expensive as nanny care mostly because it is not one-on-one care. You might also consider a neighbor who is a stay-at-home parent to look after your child for a fee. The cost should be somewhere between those for a nanny and a day care center because you take the child to the neighbor's house every day and the care is not one-on-one if she or he has children of her or his own.

After age one or two, when children are more social, a setting that allows them interaction with other children is best, especially if your child is an only child. My sister told me that it doesn't matter who is caring for your child as long as that person loves him or her. I investigated several day care facilities. The costs ranged from $750 to $1,100 per month. The one that I liked best was the least expensive one—it seemed more friendly and low-key. So, the most expensive is not necessarily the best. In a high-rent area, such as downtown, the costs will be higher, but the care may be the same or better at a lower-cost facility. The ratio of adults to infants or children is an important factor. There should be one adult for every two or three infants for the bulk of the day. (Some infant day care centers have one person starting at 6:00 a.m. and a different one arriving later but staying until 6:00 p.m., but most of the day more than one person is there.) Make sure your day care facility allows you to visit anytime. If not, perhaps you should look elsewhere.

After the initial cost of the adoption, day care is the most expensive cost of raising a preschool child. If you are single, you may have no choice but to hire someone unless you work from your home. I can barely afford the cost of day care and at the same time save for college tuition. I realize, however, that it all gets cheaper as they get older. Day care costs drop after age three at most facilities because the kids need less direct care (i.e., no more diapers, etc.). Also, when they enter preschool or kindergarten, you may need only after-school care, which is much less expensive than all-day day care. I now have a nanny who comes to my house every day and leaves when I get home. She is from Vietnam so she is teaching my boys their native language. It is a little more expensive than a day care center, but much easier on me. I don't have to take them out every day, and if they have colds (which seems to be the rule rather than the exception in winter), they can stay home and I don't have to miss work. Andy is in preschool now four days a week, so he gets some social interaction with other kids his age.

YOUR SOCIAL LIFE

How will your social life change? You may think that your social life will wither away, but it probably will not; it will just be very different. You can and will see your friends. Some friends will not be around as much as they used to be. You will, however, gain new friends, some of whom might be gay parents also. I've heard this from straight parents too. People tend to surround themselves with others who are in the same boat, going through the same motions. Your child's happiness is a reflection of your happiness, and you'll need to maintain a balance of adult social activity while caring for your child. This reminds me of the safety instructions on an airplane. They always tell you to put your oxygen mask on first, then put one on your child. The lesson here is to take care of yourself and your happiness so that you are fully capable of providing a loving and happy home for your child.

Chapter 12

How to Avoid Problems
and What to Do if They Arise

In some respects, adoption can be thought of as a merger or an acquisition, but it is certainly not the corporate type; you can't walk away from it at 6:00 p.m. every day and leave all of your troubles behind. Emotions run high, especially after you've seen a picture of your child, or even higher after you've met him or her. The application and approval process is complicated and will probably not occur without a snag or two.

The media, especially newsmagazines, love to run stories on adoptions because they have all the dramatic elements producers look for—hopes, dreams, family, international adventure, loss, and, hopefully, but not always, happy endings.

The worst case scenario is that you could prepare your home, plan a trip, venture overseas to adopt your child, and come home without him or her. This never happened to me so I cannot adequately convey the feelings related to such an occurrence, but I imagine that they would be exactly the opposite of the absolute joy I felt when I brought my sons home.

So, what do you do if you encounter a serious problem in your adoption? Of course, each problem is different and each solution is unique. In many countries, delays are almost inherent in the process, due to the nature of third world governments. However, a friend of mine recalled how the Communist government of the country where he adopted treated him and his partner well while the U.S. government denied their child's entry into the States. Thus, assumptions we make in the beginning about how the process will go are not always on target.

One of the most important rules to remember is to ask questions throughout the process, beginning with the first interview you have with an agency. The more you know, the better you will be able to solve or assist in solving problems you may encounter. Remember, knowledge is power. Ask your agency for a description of the process (which they should have in writing). Read it and inquire about items you do not understand. Keep in mind that your agency may not know the intricate details of international adoptions. They may or may not have traveled to the countries with which they work. Find out, and ask whether they have been involved in other adoptions there. They may be able to share stories of other parents' problems and help you avoid them. They may also be able to give you a better picture of the circumstances surrounding your trip. Your agency should be able to give you some references for parents who have adopted from the program you are considering. Be sure to call as many as you can and ask them what, if any, delays they faced and why. Find out whether they had to use a foreign or U.S. lawyer, or none at all. You may want to contact an immigration or adoption attorney (or both) before you leave the United States. If you do, be sure to obtain his or her e-mail address. This meeting may cost you $100 or $150 for a one-hour session, but the connection may be invaluable when you are in the foreign country and you need help.

If you can, take your own or rent a laptop computer, especially if you have not previously traveled to a third world country. You will benefit greatly from having a connection to your agency, family, and friends in the United States. Alternatively, the business center of the hotel where you are staying may have computer access, but you will incur a fee for e-mail, usually per message sent or received or for computer time. An alternative is to find a cybercafé, which are plentiful in developing countries. The fees for use of the computers at cybercafés can be less expensive than in the hotels.

When you arrive in the country, ask all the questions you have of the facilitator. You are paying that person for his or her time and you should have a clear understanding of what lies ahead for you and your new child. You should request a summary of the day-by-day events you are about to experience. If the birth mother is not involved in the adoption process, ask the facilitator for information about your child's origins. Request any documents that can substantiate his or her background, especially any medical records in addition to the ones you may have received with your referral. If the birth mother is involved, ask whether she is being reimbursed for medical expenses or lost work during pregnancy.

The more you find out now, the greater your ability to help your child understand his or her origins. Unless you are also adopted, you will not necessarily understand his or her feelings about identity issues. Any information (unless obviously harmful) can only help you and your child down the road.

It is important to note the distinction between "direct" adoptions and "state" adoptions. Direct adoptions are those in which the birth mother relinquishes her child to the adopting parents within the laws of the local government. A direct adoption must undergo all the scrutiny of any other adoption but carries with it more risks because of the obvious speculation by authorities (foreign and U.S.) that the birth mother has an incentive for giving up her baby. In a direct adoption, the birth mother must prove that she is single and that she cannot care for her child (usually due to poverty). On one hand, meeting the birth mother is a wonderful experience and it gives her the comfort of knowing who will be raising her baby. If possible, obtain a photo of her to help answer your child's inevitable questions a few years down the road.

"State" adoptions are the more common route. Most children adopted from foreign countries have been abandoned; thus, they are wards of the state and live in an orphanage. Orphanages are usually run or funded by the government. State adoptions offer little (if any) chance to meet the birth mother, but, obviously, they have fewer risks because there can be no accusation of baby buying if the birth mothers are not involved in any way.

I adopted Andy directly from his birth mother and Vincent from an orphanage. Now, knowing more about the two options, I would recommend a state adoption due to the greater transparency of the process, and because the child's need for a home can go unquestioned. The BCIS uses this specific definition of an orphan:

> *What is an Orphan?* Under U.S. immigration law, an orphan is a foreign child who does not have any parents because of the death or disappearance of, abandonment or desertion by, or separation or loss from both parents. An orphan can also be a for-

eign-born child with a sole or surviving parent who is unable to provide for the child's basic needs, consistent with the local standards of the foreign sending country, and has, in writing, irrevocably released the child for emigration and adoption.

If the child doesn't meet this definition, you may have trouble getting a U.S. visa for him or her.

Contact your local representative's or senator's office before leaving the country to let him or her know of your plans. Get an e-mail address of someone in that office who could help you if you need diplomatic assistance. If you can, visit the local or national office to put a face with your name. People are much more willing to help people they have met personally.

Money issues must also be considered, even though, given the outcome, the total amount spent may seem irrelevant. Most of us must admit that we do not have unlimited resources. Ask your agency who would pay for an attorney if one is needed (most likely it will be you). If a serious problem arises, you will need to determine whether you should remain in the country or leave without your child and work on your adoption form the United States. This is where an attorney may be able to help you. Ask about refunds in the event that the adoption does not go through. If you have a contract with your agency, this topic should be addressed there. Obviously, this is a tough question, one that we don't want to think about, but if the adoption doesn't go through, which happens occasionally, your pain will be somewhat reduced if you receive a prompt refund of some of the funds you've spent. This will provide you with resources to focus on filing an appeal or trying again, if that is what you decide to do.

If asked whether you are gay, you should under no circumstances lie to any government official, U.S. or foreign. If you are uncomfortable saying yes, and you think the question is beyond the scope of that government official's duties, you can simply say, "As a matter of principle, I choose not to answer that question." Most U.S. officials with whom you'll have contact (i.e., those in the BCIS or U.S. embassy) are not allowed to ask if you are gay.

Chapter 13

My Decision to Adopt Again

I grew up in a family of six kids, three boys and three girls. We were the Brady Bunch in our neighborhood, although our family was not formed the same way as Mike and Carol's. Having grown up in a big family, I don't know what it is like to be an only child. My connections to my siblings have been and will continue to be strong. About two years after adopting Andy, I thought about how his life as an only child would be when he is older, not just at eight years old, but at fifteen, twenty-five, and forty.

The idea of having another child had always appealed to me but seemed out of my reach, for several reasons, the biggest of which was my sanity. Would I go crazy having two toddlers by myself? Would I be able to handle the day-to-day chores, such as grocery shopping, cleaning, and cooking? Would I ever be able to get out of the house? I realized these were the same questions I had asked myself three years earlier. Since I often told others that adopting Andy was the best thing I ever did, I had to believe that if I truly wanted a second child, it would happen and would eventually work out in the end.

Another reason for my hesitancy was money. I knew I would have to borrow to pay for half of the adoption costs, and that day care would be more costly with two. Thinking it was now or never, I opted to take on a little debt.

The third reason, and probably the biggest unknown at that time, was logistics. I thought about when the kids become teenagers and I have to coordinate their soccer game pickups, parties, and so forth. On the cover of a recent issue of *Newsweek* was the cover story headline "Is Juggling Your Kids' Sports, Music and Homework Burning You Out?" I was sure to face just such a situation, and though I can solicit my family members and friends to help, that becomes burdensome after a while. After all, they have lives too. The real solution, I thought then and still do now, is to have a partner who is willing to help, but that is a story for another book.

My first thought about having a second child was, "Am I doing this just for Andy?" I struggled with the answer. I chose to think of my decision to adopt again as simply expanding my family. I wanted kids (in the plural) running around my house, and I had a home and a lot of love to give to another child. Andy, of course, would benefit, and my new child would have a great brother. Also, although it was not the main reason, adopting again would satisfy some basic philanthropic needs of mine. My heart sinks when I see children in need and I feel I can help one or two of them. So I had several reasons to adopt again, and several reasons not to adopt again, but the former list was greater. I knew in my heart that it was the right thing to do with my life.

Another thought I had concerning adopting again involved entertainment. I believed that some of the pressure of entertaining a child would be removed by adopting again. Andy and his brother would be able to entertain each other, have fun together, or at least share some good old-fashioned sibling rivalry to spice up their lives.

As I traveled to Vietnam for the third time, I wrote a journal again. The following entries reveal some of my feelings about adopting a second child.

Saturday, May 12, 2001

I am writing this on an airplane, which seems to be the only time to write anymore. Airplanes make me very emotional, which allows a bit more feelings to come through. I can't explain why airplanes make my eyes tear up, but I think it is the fact that they are either taking you from or to the ones you love. I have just left Andy at my brother's house and from there he will be staying at my sister's house and then back home for a week while my friend Bob watches him. I'll be gone for eighteen days and this is the longest we've been apart since I adopted him. I am on my way to Asia for work for two weeks, then down to Saigon to meet my new son. This trip is much different from the last time I did this. I am worried—very worried. I know I was worried on the first trip and maybe more than I am now, but it just feels different. I am worried for several reasons. One is that I fear that something will go wrong. There has been a flurry of activity in Vietnam recently about baby-buying scandals and INS denials, mostly surrounding direct adoptions. I am adopting from an orphanage, so I do not think I will have that trouble, but one can never be sure until you board the plane home with your new child. The second reason I am worried is day care. I do not have a plan yet. I will probably bring the baby home in a couple of months. I have a couple of options for Andy, but not for the baby. I would like to hire a nanny (preferably a Vietnamese nanny) to come to my house daily. That way, I would not have to bundle the boys up daily to take them to one or possibly two locations. When I adopted before, it all fell into place so I am confident that it will again this time. My sister-in-law, Jody, reassured me yesterday that my worries are natural for any big life-changing event such as this.

My other worry is whether or not I will have a placement by the time I leave Vietnam. I think the facilitator is working on this, but as of now, I have no referral. Whoever my referral is, I am worried that he will not be a good baby or a good toddler. I have been blessed with a child who never had his terrible twos and is so sweet and loving. Everyone around him comments as such. If Andy were not such a well-behaved little boy, I do not think I would be adopting again. I fear that my second child will be just the opposite, but these are the risks one takes when adopting (or even when having a biological child).

I am flying in to Saigon again. I am feeling a bit unsettled about this trip. I am hoping that I can handle two kids. I really want two, but I know it will be a lot of work. Everyone around me is encouraging me and those who have two kids say that I will never regret it. I wrote a note to a friend the other day about this and I said that the paperwork has all been filed for this adoption and at this point, it is something that is happening to me—it is out of my control. I am sure everything will be fine, but I still have my reservations.

I have never been in an orphanage before. I am looking forward to it in some ways, but not in others. I think it will break my heart to see all of the children, especially the older ones who need homes but may not be placed because most adopting parents want infants.

After checking in at the hotel, Loan (the adopting parents' escort) and I traveled about a half an hour to the orphanage. We were held up at the gate for about ten minutes and I sat quietly, but not so patiently, in the backseat of the van. I was about to meet my second child so I briefed Loan on how to use the video camera and my regular camera. I wanted to have a recording of my first meeting of my child like I did with Andy. We waited in a waiting area for about fifteen minutes, where they served us tea. Loan said, at first, they would not let me in the orphanage because it was Saturday. She persuaded them instead to bring Le Tu Anh out to meet his new father. One of the caregivers walked in with a tiny baby. She handed him to me and I immediately thought he was very small for four months. He was very cute—he had great features and a nice complexion. The shirt he was wearing was torn and frayed; it was basically worn out from being used over and over by many infants. He had scabies on his arm and formula in his hair. He was fragile and seemed like a newborn to me rather than a baby who, just one day before, had had his four-month birthday. Also, he seemed troubled in some way that I cannot describe. He was not crying or fussy, just silent and unanimated. I held him for about forty-five minutes as there was nowhere to set him down. We then decided to go on about the day's other business and leave Le Tu Anh to take his afternoon nap. This meeting was so different from the first meeting with Andy. I got to take Andy to my hotel with me for two nights when we first met.

We spent most of the rest of the day in the van. We had to travel about an hour to visit the family of a seven year-old little girl who was being adopted by a woman in Iowa and then to Vung Tau to an orphanage. The seven-year-old little girl has juvenile arthritis, I think. Loan did not know the English name of her disease. Her family was very poor and there were lots of kids running around. The little girl was about half the height of most seven-year-old girls. There was another smaller girl there and because the sick little girl couldn't walk very far, the smaller girl would pick her up and walk around with her on her hip. I am sure it will be difficult to separate these two girls if the little girl is adopted. The sick girl sat in my lap for a long time. She seemed content even though you could tell she was in pain. She probably didn't know life without pain. We left them with some food and money to buy more. For me it was a sad day to see people living in such dire circumstances. Dirt and smell were everywhere. But I constantly have to remind myself that they do not know a different life and that is evident in their apparent happiness.

We then traveled to an orphanage at Vung Tau, which is near the South China Sea. We got to the orphanage but were not allowed in because it was a weekend, so Loan had to find the director's house and deliver some paperwork. We then drove to the seashore, mostly because I said something about being this close we might as well take a look at the ocean. It is a beautiful resort town with fishing boats in the sea and mountainous islands and peninsulas as their backdrop. It reminds me of the book *My Father's Boat,* which I read to Andy quite often (and it brings a tear to my eye every time). The book is about a Vietnamese father and son in America and the boy's grandfather who is still in Vietnam. They are a family of fishermen separated by the war.

We traveled along the coast for a few miles and it was beautiful. We then traveled back to Saigon, which was about two hours away, but seemed like three or four hours. I was miserably tired when we got back to the hotel at 8:00 p.m., but I can't imagine how tired the driver was. Driving in Vietnam must be very difficult.

Sunday, May 13, 2001

I went shopping today, and in the afternoon, I met with the foster caregiver of Andy who cared for him three years ago. It was a good day, even though in the back of my mind were thoughts about the baby and how he seemed unhealthy. I am not sleeping very well these nights. I wake up and worry about the baby and this whole process.

Tuesday, May 15, 2001

Today, Loan and I traveled again to the orphanage. We brought a big bag of toys that I got at the Tax Market the day before. When we got there we were asked to wait in the waiting area and we were told that I could not enter the orphanage because my dossier was not here yet. They said they would not bring my baby to see me. Then, they showed me the medical report for the baby, Le Tu Anh. At first, I did not notice it, but the last blood test on the report showed that he has tested positive for hepatitis B. What to do next, I do not know. What does it mean? I used to know the differences between the hepatitis diseases A, B, and C but am drawing a blank now. I felt that my gut feeling when holding him three days earlier was correct. He has been ill and that may have had something to do with his growth in the last four months. I have to be really honest with myself about adopting a healthy child. Because I am a single parent, I feel I cannot knowingly make a decision to adopt a child with special needs. Some people out there are able to handle that, but I do not feel that I can. I feel that this is one of those personal decisions, like deciding to adopt trans-racially, or whether to adopt a boy or a girl, or even what to name your child. Others cannot make these decisions. The same goes with deciding to adopt a child with special needs. I remembered back to what I said in my homestudy meetings. I indicated then my desire for a healthy child, so I decided to stay with that plan.

Loan and I took a copy of the medical report, left the toys for the older kids, and left the orphanage without seeing the baby. I felt a sense of sadness for the baby Le Tu Anh, but also a sense of relief because I was scared to take a baby about which I had an adverse gut feeling. I know it sounds cruel, but I must be realistic. When you visit a country like Vietnam and there are armless, legless, or burned children in the streets begging, you soon realize that you can't save the world. This experience softens me, as I am quick to give money to these kids, but it also hardens me because I have made a decision not to take a sick child home with me, and while that feels justified, it also feels cruel.

Loan and I discussed strategy in the taxi back to the hotel. A few hours later, I could call the adoption facilitator in Virginia, as it would be morning there. After a few phone calls and a fax back and forth, she assigned to me a baby boy from the orphanage in Vung Tau, the village on the South China Sea we had visited days earlier. An awful day had a happy ending. I was scheduled to meet my new son-to-be on Thursday morning. They were bringing him to my hotel at 8:00 a.m. I did not have a picture of him, I just knew he was a five-month-old boy.

Thursday, May 17, 2001

I was eating breakfast with some new friends, Ellen and Richard (who were in the process of adopting a four-month-old boy), when Loan came running into the breakfast area and said, "Kevin, your new baby is here." I was almost complacent about this one because I had been on a bit of a roller coaster since arriving in Vietnam. I went to the lobby of the hotel and there was an older woman sitting there with a very healthy-looking five-month-old baby. I hoped that was him, and I realized it was as Loan walked me toward them. In all of the confusion and people approaching her, she didn't know who the new parent was, so she did not hand him to me. I just stared at him and marveled at how handsome he is. Wow, I have that feeling again. This one is it, and he'll be my son, if all goes well from here. We sat in the lobby and Richard went to his room for his guitar. He came down to the lobby to sing to my new son. He sang "Here Comes the Sun" but changed the words to "Here Comes Your Son." I cried. Loan was videotaping the whole scene, so it is now recorded on tape that I cry easily.

We then went to my room and I talked to Lan, the baby's caregiver, through Loan's translation. She has cared for him since he was five days old. She sometimes sleeps overnight at the orphanage. I think that is why he is so healthy. He is in an orphanage but has not received typical orphanage care. I am looking forward to coming back to get him. I hope to spend a few days at the village of Vung Tau when I return to Vietnam so that I will have a frame of reference of where he came from. Lan said that his birth mother was eighteen years old when she had him and could not keep him because she was very poor and single. She sells lottery tickets on the street. I asked if there was a picture of her in the orphanage with his paperwork, and Lan said that there might be. I have a picture of Andy's birth mom and will not know what to do when they start asking about their moms and I have a picture of one, but not the other. I spent three hours with my new son and it was great. He is full of life, seems very content, and is absolutely beautiful. I feel very lucky again. Probably the best part of the turn of events is that I was able to meet him and leave that evening without filing paperwork. He is from a province that requires only one trip, so I did not have to stay for what might have been another week. I have already been away from Andy for almost three weeks, so I really feel the need to get home. I feel ready for adopting my second son. I do not have the anxiety that I had only a week ago. It feels just like it did with Andy. I knew it when I held him that he was destined to be my son and Andy's brother.

I left Saigon and got home a day later. Andy was waiting at the airport with my brother and sister and their families. It was a great reunion. I can't imagine what my life would be like without him.

Thursday, July 19, 2001

Today I am traveling back to Vietnam via Hong Kong with my sister-in-law, Jody.

Sunday, July 22, 2001

It is Sunday morning and we're up at 5:00 a.m. We are going to Vung Tau today to get the baby and stay there for a few days. The Giving and Receiving ceremony that was set for Monday is now delayed until Tuesday or Wednesday, but at least we'll be able to have the baby the whole time down there. We spent the day yesterday arriving in the morning from Hong Kong and then with my friend John and his twin boys, Joshua and Jonathan. They are so cute. Saigon seems the same as it was a few years ago but it is the end of the rainy season, so we got a couple of showers yesterday. We're also suffering from jet lag and caffeine loading to compensate, which doesn't always work. John got a baby-sitter last night, so we went out to dinner on the rooftop of the Rex Hotel.

Monday, July 23, 2001

We are in Vung Tau now. It is Monday morning. We feel like vagabonds, as we haven't spent two nights in the same place since we arrived in Asia. We went to the orphanage yesterday and met with Vincent but were not able to take him with us. We are now supposed to have the G&R today, but it may be delayed if the vice minister is not back from his weekend away. Vincent is so cute and healthy and seems happy, although he didn't know who was this guy making a big fuss over him. We went to the beach yesterday for a little while. There must have been an oil spill lately, so we only waded. It is beautiful here, but just not very clean close up. John will pick up his visas for the twins tomorrow at the consulate so he is ready to go, but he is waiting until Friday for his planned flights. (He is so happy being busy.) The drive to Vung Tau was a rough one. We saw an accident between two motorbikes and an ox cart. The oxen ran away and lots of people followed them but left the injured guy by the side of the road. We wait today at the hotel for the scoop on the Giving and Receiving ceremony.

Thursday, July 26, 2001

Well, I have Vincent here in our hotel room, although I still have not had my Giving and Receiving ceremony. Possession is nine-tenths of the law in the United States, isn't it? The G&R is supposed to be tomorrow, Friday morning, but I am not convinced. Today we were supposed to leave Ho Chi Minh City for Vung Tau at 11:00 but didn't leave until 1:30; thus, by the time we got there and picked up the baby, the Ministry of Justice was closed. So, I go back tomorrow. I have him, so I am much happier than I was yesterday. This process is just like it was with Andy, but different players.

Friday, July 27, 2001

Well, I am a daddy again. We finally had the G&R today at 3:30. Five days late, but hey, who's counting? I built in a few extra days because I knew everything would not go as planned. Vincent is more animated now that he is out of the orphanage. He has had his first crawl on carpet, his first bath with running water, his first look in a mirror, and his first viewing of TV. He is having a good time and getting quite used to us. He spent the day with Jody and I went to Vung Tau, again! I was there all day in the heat with three other adopting women, one of which had her baby with her. We had a nice time despite the anxiety of not knowing if we'd be able to accomplish our mission (we didn't want to wait the weekend and lose more days). We had the best lunch today in a brothel/restaurant/bar in Vung Tau. (Prostitution is the number two industry in Vung Tau behind shipping.) It was the middle of the day and on the other side of the restaurant there was a table of Russian and Chinese comrades (who were drinking a lot) and Vietnamese girls. We joked that they were about to make what we were trying to adopt. There were only two tables occupied in the whole restaurant and there were no further extremes I could think of. The only commonality was that we all ordered food, which was very good. As we waited for hours for our facilitator, the madam of the place approached and spoke through our waiter, who translated. She said she wanted me to be her brother for the night. I just smiled.

We'll visit the INS on Monday, hopefully. Then the other stuff is a formality. I can't imagine what we'd do if there weren't other families here adopting. They are such a comfort when we have a delay or a snag. Everybody seems to be getting on planes with their babies, so we are keeping that in mind while we are going through the difficult process.

Monday, July 30, 2001

Today, I went to pick up Vincent's medical report and Jody stayed behind at the hotel with Vincent. I had previously told my adoption facilitator that I'd like to meet Vincent's birth mother if possible, but not before getting his visa (because, sometimes, the INS or consulate officials ask if you've met the birth mother, and if you have, eyebrows are raised). While I was out getting the medical report, she apparently came to the hotel. Jody recognized her from the picture that I had and saw her in the lobby. She kept looking at Vincent. It must have been difficult for her to see Vincent with another woman and not be able to approach her. Perhaps she was shy about the language barrier. Jody called me on Loan's cell phone and asked what she should do. I told her to stay in the lobby and if someone does help translate, let her hold him for a little while and possibly get some pictures. Well, there was no one to translate and Vincent's birth mother left in the afternoon without meeting Jody. I feel sad that she did not meet Jody or me because we would have assured her that we'd take good care of him. I hope to arrange a meeting after I get the visa.

Wednesday, August 1, 2001

Vincent has been a little under the weather. He's had a low-grade temperature the last few days and a runny nose. We've been to the British/Australian medical clinic a couple of times now. He has developed a boil on his bottom (or bum as they are calling it). It is painful and makes him generally miserable. The doctor at the clinic told us today that this type of thing is very common in the tropics, mostly due to the heat. Plus I think he's also not used to wearing diapers. The doctor said plainly, "Diapers cause diaper rash." The orphanage kept most of the babies in cloth swaddle wraps. We have been keeping the diaper off as much as possible in the room, which is a little bit insane. Baths with warm water seem to make him feel much better.

We went on a dinner river cruise last night. It goes up and down the Saigon River. We got to see some of the shipping areas and the skyline of the city. Poor Vinnie. All we've been doing since he's been with us is give him drops of medicine and put ointments on him that sting. He probably wants to go back to his same-old-same-old life at the orphanage. I think he'll be glad he hooked up with me someday— just not sure how soon.

Thursday, August 2, 2001

Well, yesterday we had a scare. The INS called and asked us to come over for an interview after we thought we'd filed all the proper paperwork the day before. So we went and the guy was cold as ice. (Isn't this supposed to be a happy event?) He kept asking if anyone else lived in my house (like a partner). I said, no, it is only me and Andy and he still asked again. "Are you sure no one else lives with you?" I almost asked him which part of "no" do you not understand? However, there must have been no problem with my adoption because I called the INS office later in the afternoon and he had approved my case. Yahoo! So, we are going to the U.S. consulate today for another interview (should just be a formality) and we can hopefully leave tomorrow.

Vinnie still has his boil, so we're going back to the doctor today.

Friday, August 3, 2001

We got Vincent's immigrant visa today! It is Friday evening about 5:00 p.m. We'll fly home tomorrow. Within forty-eight hours, I'll be able to introduce Vincent to his big brother, Andy. I tried to meet with his birth mother, but she apparently could not come to Saigon today. I hope to find her somehow and send her some pictures of Vincent from time to time.

Throughout all of the process for my second adoption, I was concerned about the transition for Andy and Vincent. In hindsight, they did great—it was me who had a rough time. I was on paternity leave for one month before my nanny started. The month off turned out to be beneficial for all three of us. I was there to explain all the baby stuff to Andy and he was willing to "help" me. I got a touch of cabin fever, so we took a short vacation in North Carolina. When the nanny started and I returned to work, I soon realized I needed a balance in my life. As much as I love my kids, I also enjoy going to work and would probably not do well as a stay-at-home parent. I admire those who do stay home to raise their children.

After being home from Vietnam with Vincent for about six months, I have to say that I understand all of my reservations and why the decision to adopt again was so difficult. I look back now with no regrets. I have two beautiful, kind, loving sons. I am an influence in their lives. They depend on me. My life is enriched. Many people say that they are lucky, but, clearly, I am the lucky one.

Chapter 14

Life with Kids

"How do you manage with two kids?" "Do you ever get time for yourself?" "You certainly have your hands full." "You must be exhausted." "Must be a lot of work."

These are some of the questions and comments I get from people I meet. I answer that I am simply doing what millions of people have done for many thousands of years—raising kids. My life with my children, on a day-to-day basis, feels more natural than my life before kids. I do not find it exhausting, or something I have to manage; it is indeed full of work, but it is gratifying work.

I call our routine a rhythm. On weekday mornings I awake at about 6:45 a.m. and can usually get my shower before the kids wake up. But if they are already awake, I put them on my bed to watch cartoons while I get ready. We then eat breakfast (cereal and yogurt), and the nanny comes at about 7:15. I still get the newspaper and try to read some of it during breakfast. I'm off to work at 7:30. Andy goes to pre-school from 9:00 to 12:00 Monday, Tuesday, Wednesday, and Thursday. They have lunch at 12:30 or so and are down for their naps at about 1:30. I arrive home at 5:00 p.m. to relieve the nanny. In the early evenings, they watch PBS *(Arthur, Clifford, Dragon Tales)* while I cook dinner. We eat at about 6:30 and I finish cleaning up at about 7:30. Then we play, watch a movie, or read stories. Sometimes we go for a walk or shopping or to the grocery store. I do not feel confined to the house because I have two kids. I run errands with them just as often as I used to before I had them. At about 8:15 or 8:30, it is bath time. Vincent is usually out first because he has to have his bottle before going to bed. Andy likes to play in the tub a little longer. Then, if we have time, we read a couple of stories and they are in the sack by 9:00 p.m. They both fall asleep pretty well now, but at first, Vincent had to be in a separate bedroom because he'd cry before falling asleep. They are now in the same room—Vincent in Andy's old crib and Andy in his big-boy bed.

On the weekends, we can lounge around a bit more. Andy usually walks into my room about 7:00 and Vincent makes it known verbally that he doesn't want to be left behind in their room by himself. I get him out of his crib and they watch cartoons in my room until about 8:00 or so. We are then up for breakfast and whatever we have planned for the day. If it is nice outside, we go to the park, or on a bike ride. I have a trailer for my bike that fits two kids. We usually stop along the way at a park that has swings and climbing equipment. Sometimes we stay home and just clean the house or work in the yard. They take their naps at about 2:00 p.m., and in the evening, we might go out to dinner with friends or just hang around the house. In the late evenings, between 9:00 and 11:00 p.m., I have what I call my free time, and I usually do some brainless activity, such as watching TV or a rented movie.

So, that is our schedule. Raising two kids is just a matter of prioritizing your daily routine to make room for a little dependent (or two). Now that Andy is getting older and he can carry on a conversation, our world has opened up immensely. It is so rewarding to watch him become a big little boy with his own thoughts and ideas. He asks for hugs often, during which he says softly, "I love my daddy." He seems proud of being from Vietnam and seems already to have a strong self-identity. Vincent watches Andy closely and imitates much of what he sees. He is now starting to speak. "Da-da" and "thank you" were his first words.

It is not always quiet at our house. At times I am frustrated. Vincent is at the age where he likes to undo everything, having a natural ability to take apart what I've just finished putting together, such as redistributing toys I've picked up or emptying the just loaded dishwasher. I guess he just wants to be close to me. Sometimes, if they are both whining and too loud for me, I just leave the room and go to another room and sit on the floor. In a matter of minutes, they've found me and are climbing all over me. We soon forget our frustrations. I choose my battles. I can say, "No" or "Stop that" or "Don't scream anymore, please!" only so many times. In general, they are smart, good-natured, typically curious boys.

I knew that it was going to be difficult in the beginning with two kids, especially two with different agendas (food requirements, nap schedules, safety concerns, etc.). In reality, though, it is manageable. I know from raising Andy thus far that it does get easier as they get older. I remember an evening at church after Vincent had just started walking. Following mass, during the social hour, I was able to put him down and let him walk around a bit. I had never been able to do that before because he would get dirty crawling around. I said to myself, "Great, it just got easier!" Such milestones mark the moments your life becomes easier, such as, when they can hold their own bottle and eat on their own with utensils. Andy now hangs his coat on a hook when coming in from outside and puts his shoes away (most often without being told).

Notice that in this chapter, the word "gay," until now, did not appear once. To me, that is testimony to the belief that sexual orientation has nothing to do with parenting. When I started my first adoption, I heard this from the agency that did my homestudy. I believe it now more than ever.

Afterword

It has been almost a year since I finished writing this book. Not much has changed except that school and all that goes with it is drawing nearer. Andy will enter kindergarten and Vincent will enter pre-school in the fall. We'll soon find ourselves immersed in schoolwork, soccer, and social calendars (theirs, not mine). I consider our family to be pretty doggone normal, even though I am a single gay man, my kids were born in another country, and there is no mom in the picture.

But, what strikes me most after reading this book once again is that I believe gay men are on the edge of a unique place in today's society. Some are having kids through surrogacy or coparenting, but most gay men are becoming dads through adoption. We are not choosing adoption as a second choice because of fertility issues. Rather, with open arms we are traveling overseas or across state lines to create a family. And, we are doing it with a lot of forethought. Once we adopt, we are good at being fathers. It's an unexpected turn of events, but certainly apropos that these men who want to be parents and children who need parents are coming together with such enthusiasm. I can't think of a better example of a win-win situation.

Maybe it's because we are gay, and naturally liberal toward alternative families that allows us to unconditionally love a child that is not biologically our own. Maybe we just feel privileged to be given the chance to raise a child. Maybe it's because we were never able to just assume we were going to be parents, but had to work at it. Whatever the reason, we are crazy about our kids. I recently heard of a woman who unexpectedly got pregnant during her senior year in college. She and the father married and had the baby. They were wondering why their little boy had such serious behavior problems. I realized then that children can read our emotions and my kids are happy and pretty well behaved because I was really ready for them. I have suggested in this book that fatherhood is easier than I thought it would be. I think it is easy for me because I wanted it so badly. Fatherhood is not for every guy, but for some of us it fits, it works, and the rewards are terrific.

Appendix

Helpful Web Sites and Listservs

WEB SITES

- Human Rights Campaign—FamilyNet (probably the most comprehensive Web site for gay parenting):
  <www.hrc.org/familynet/>

- Single-parent adopting:
  Adopting on Your Own
  <www.adoptingonyourown.com>

- General adoption Web sites:
  <www.adopting.com>
  <www.adoption.com>
  <www.adoptablekids.com>
  <www.kidsave.org>

- Surrogacy:
  Growing Generations
  <www.growinggenerations.com>

- Magazines:
  Gay Parent Magazine
  <www.gayparentmag.com>
  Fathering Magazine (for fathers in general)
  <www.fathermag.com>

- General:
  Family Pride Coalition (advocacy group)
  <www.familypride.org>
  COLAGE: Children of Lesbians and Gays Everywhere

<www.COLAGE.org>
National Adoption Information Clearinghouse
<www.calib.com/naic/>

- Government:
    Bureau of Citizenship and Immigration Services (under
    the Department of Homeland Security), formerly the INS
    <www.bcis.gov> or <www.immigration.gov>
    U.S. Department of State International Adoption:
    <http://travel.state.gov/adopt.html>
    Office of Children's Issues:
    <http://travel.state.gov/officeofchildissues.html>

LISTSERVS

Listservs are computer bulletin boards for people with a common interest. For instance, the Vietnam Adoption Listserv is subscribed to by people
interested in adopting or who have already adopted from Vietnam. Much
can be learned from other peoples' stories and experiences, and you can ask
questions of people who might have the answers.

- China Adoption Listserv
    Send an e-mail to:
      a-parents-china-subscribe@yahoogroups.com
      In the body of the message, type the following command:
        SUBSCRIBE

- Guatemala Adoption Listserv
    Send an e-mail to:
      LISTSERV@MAELSTROM.STJOHNS.EDU
      In the body of the message, type the following command:
        SUBSCRIBE GUATEMALA-ADOPT

- Russia Adoption Listserv
    Go to <www.frua.org> (Families for Russian and Ukrainian
    Adoptions) Scroll down and enter your name and e-mail address
      Choose subscribe and press UPDATE

- Ukraine Adoption Listserv
    Send an e-mail to:
      Adoption_from_Ukraine-subscribe@yahoogroups.com
      In the body of the message, type the following command:
        SUBSCRIBE

- Vietnam Adoption Listserv
    Send an e-mail to:
        APV-request@mamnon.org
        In the body of the message, type the following command:
        SUBSCRIBE

- Gay Adoption Listserv
    Send an e-mail to:
        LISTSERV@MAELSTROM.STJOHNS.EDU
        In the body of the message, type the following command:
        SUBSCRIBE GAY-APARENT

- Discussion on Cross-Cultural Adoption Listserv
    Send an e-mail to:
        LISTSERV@MAELSTROM.STJOHNS. EDU
        In the body of the message, type the following command:
        SUBSCRIBE XCULTUREADOPT

- Single Parents Listserv
    Send an e-mail to:
        LISTSERV@MAELSTROM.STJOHNS.EDU
        In the body of the message, type the following command:
        subscribe SINGLE-APARENT

30.